SIMPLY STYLISH
SLIMMER
RECIPES

❧

CAROLYN HUMPHRIES

foulsham
LONDON • NEW YORK • TORONTO • SYDNEY

foulsham

The Publishing House, Bennetts Close,
Cippenham, Slough, Berkshire, SL1 5AP, England

ISBN 0-572-02499-1

Printed in Great Britain by Cox & Wyman Ltd, Reading

CONTENTS

INTRODUCTION

◎

Would you like a diet that means you can eat three good meals a day, including puddings, plus snacks in between *and* a gin and tonic or glass of wine if you fancy it? A diet that includes sinful foods like garlic bread, profiteroles and chocolate mousse? A diet where you don't have to spend hours with a calculator adding up the calories? A diet packed with recipes so sensational you can even serve them for dinner parties and still lose weight? A diet where all the recipes are simple and easy to make, using lots of convenience foods for quickness? Well, now you have it. *Simply Stylish Slimmer Recipes* is a book for anyone and everyone who loves food and isn't prepared to sacrifice the joys of eating in order to shed the pounds. This book offers you the chance to eat better than you ever have and become the new slender you – pleasurably.

Using the book
This book can help you only if you use it for every meal. It's no good having breakfast and lunch from it, then dashing out and scoffing down a cream tea in the afternoon!

To lose weight, you need to take in less energy (calories) from food and drink than your body burns up. An average man burns about 2500 calories a day, a woman around 1900. If you have just a few pounds to lose, you could choose a fairly low-calorie intake – say 1500 for a man, 1000 for a woman: if it's a more long-term aim, then take it slowly – say 1900 for a man and 1500 for a woman.

All the recipes are divided into calorie groups, like breakfasts at 150 calories or less or light lunches at 300 calories or less and so on. You simply choose foods from groups that add up to the total calorie count you require. And as the calorie counts are often lower than the maximum for the group you will normally be well within your plan.

Drinking

Booze means calories. They are not included. If you assume for the sake of your diet that a single measure of any spirit, a small glass of wine or sherry or half a pint of beer is 100 calories and when you add up your menu you have enough to spare, then by all means have a drink or two. But just remember, if you go out and have a couple of double gin and tonics, it could be almost half your daily calorie allowance! And on no account should you substitute alcohol for proper food.

HEALTHY EATING

◎

You should never go on a deprivation diet. You must get a healthy balance of all the essential nutrients if you are to stay fit and healthy, so every day make sure you have:

- Starchy carbohydrates for energy. Eat plenty. Contrary to popular belief, they will not pile on the pounds: it is the fat or sugary stuff you add to them that makes you fat. The best sources are bread (all types), pasta, rice, cereals (including breakfast cereals, but choose wholegrain varieties, not sugar-coated ones), and potatoes.

- Proteins for body growth and repair. Eat 2 or 3 small portions a day. The best sources are fish, lean meat, poultry, dairy produce, eggs, pulses and vegetable proteins like tofu and quorn.

- Vitamins and minerals for general well-being and vitality. Eat at least 5 portions a day of fruit and vegetables to ensure you get enough. Fresh is best but frozen or canned in water or natural juices are fine too.

- Fats (the dieter's enemy) for warmth and energy. Your body gets all it needs naturally in other foods so keep fats and oils for spreading and cooking to a minimum; grill (broil) rather than fry (sauté); eat only lean meat and do not eat poultry skin.

- Fibre for healthy body functioning. Eat plenty of fruit, vegetables, wholegrain cereals and the skin on potatoes.

YOUR SLIMMING STORECUPBOARD

Keep a well-stocked kitchen and you will always be able to cook what you fancy from this book.

Flavour Enhancers
Tomato purée (paste)
Passata (sieved tomatoes)
Dried herbs: mixed (essential), mint, oregano, rosemary, basil, thyme, bay leaves, dill (dill weed), bouquet garni
Garlic: fresh, powder, granules or tube of purée (paste)
Black pepper (preferably in a grinder) and salt
Mustard: Dijon and English
Vinegar: red or white wine or cider
Reduced sugar and salt tomato ketchup (catsup)
Worcestershire sauce
Tabasco sauce
Soy sauce
Stock cubes: vegetable (essential), chicken and beef
Spices, ground: nutmeg, cayenne or chilli, cinnamon, mixed (apple-pie) spice, cumin and coriander (cilantro)
Curry paste or powder
Olive and/or sunflower oil (but to use very sparingly and only occasionally)
Artificial sweetener granules (the sort that can be used spoon-for-spoon for sweetening, but to a ratio of 1 part granules to 10 parts sugar for cooking)
Dried skimmed milk (non-fat dry milk)
Fruit juices: lemon, pure orange and apple

Canny Convenience
In water or natural juice, avoid added sugar
Tomatoes
Tuna in brine or water (not oil)
Crab
Sardines
Sweetcorn (corn)
Red kidney beans
Fruit
Consommé
Baked beans

Fridge and Freezer Specials
Medium eggs
Reduced-fat Cheddar cheese
Grated Parmesan cheese
Low-fat spread (suitable for baking and spreading)
Light (reduced-calorie) mayonnaise
Frozen peas
Frozen prawns (shrimp)
Fresh parsley (freeze and use from frozen)

Favourite Fillers
Pasta (any shapes or strands)
Long-grain rice
Plain (all-purpose) flour
Baking powder
Cornflour (cornstarch)
Part-baked French sticks
Low-calorie crispbreads
Pitta breads

Vital Veggies
Onions
Potatoes
Carrots
Salad stuffs

NOTES ON THE RECIPES

- Do not mix metric, imperial and American measures. Follow one set only in a recipe.

- American terms are given in brackets.

- All spoon measures are level: 1 tsp = 5 ml
  1 tbsp = 15 ml.

- Eggs are medium unless otherwise stated. If you use a different size, adjust the amount of other added liquid to obtain the right consistency when necessary.

- Always wash, peel, core and seed, if necessary, fresh produce before use.

- Seasoning and the use of strongly flavoured ingredients, such as onions and garlic, are very much a matter of personal taste. Taste the food as you cook and adjust the seasoning to suit your own taste.

- Always use fresh herbs unless dried are specifically called for. You can substitute dried for fresh, but use half the quantity or less as they are very pungent. Chopped frozen varieties are much better than dried. There is no substitute for fresh coriander (cilantro) or parsley for garnishing.

- Use whatever kitchen gadgets you like to speed up preparation and cooking times: mixers for whisking, food processors for grating, slicing, mixing, kneading or puréeing, blenders for liquidising.

- Always preheat the oven (unless using a fan-assisted one) and cook on the centre shelf unless otherwise stated.

- All ovens vary, so cooking times are approximate. Adjust times and temperatures to suit your appliance, especially if you have a fan oven.

- All calorie counts are per average portion and include any serving suggestions given in the recipes.

- Make sure the low-fat spread you use is suitable for cooking as well as spreading (check the label).

- Choose very low-fat or virtually fat-free varieties of dairy produce, where possible.

SOUPS AND STARTERS

All these soups and starters can also double as light meals. If you want to include a good-sized bread roll or chunk of French stick with any of them, add on an extra 150 calories. If you fancy a side salad with them, simply give yourself a pile of any salad leaves, cucumber, tomato, celery and/or grated carrot. Dress with a little lemon juice and lots of black pepper and don't worry about adding on any calories – there are so few they won't matter!

Fragrant Courgette and Tomato Soup

SERVES 4	METRIC	IMPERIAL	AMERICAN
Low-fat spread	25 g	1 oz	2 tbsp
Onion, finely chopped	1	1	1
Courgettes (zucchini), grated	4	4	4
Garlic clove, crushed	1	1	1
Vegetable stock, made with 2 stock cubes	600 ml	1 pt	2½ cups
Can of tomatoes	400 g	14 oz	1 large
Tomato purée (paste)	15 ml	1 tbsp	1 tbsp
Salt and freshly ground black pepper			
Chopped basil leaves	30 ml	2 tbsp	2 tbsp
Very low-fat fromage frais	20 ml	4 tsp	4 tsp
Small basil sprigs	4	4	4

1 Melt the low-fat spread in a large saucepan. Add the onion and cook, stirring, for 2 minutes.

2 Add the courgettes and garlic and cook, stirring, for 4 minutes.

3 Add the stock, tomatoes and tomato purée and bring to the boil, stirring. Part-cover, reduce the heat and simmer for 15 minutes.

4 Season to taste and add the chopped basil. Ladle into warmed bowls and top each with 5 ml/1 tsp fromage frais and a basil sprig.

PREPARATION TIME:
5 MINUTES

COOKING TIME:
25 MINUTES

CALORIES: LESS THAN 100

Smooth Cheese Soup

SERVES 4	METRIC	IMPERIAL	AMERICAN
Large potato, diced	1	1	1
Large carrot, diced	1	1	1
Small onion, diced	1	1	1
Celery stick, diced	1	1	1
Vegetable stock, made with 2 stock cubes	600 ml	1 pt	2½ cups
Dried mixed herbs	2.5 ml	½ tsp	½ tsp
Low-fat Cheddar cheese, grated	100 g	4 oz	1 cup
Skimmed milk	150 ml	¼ pt	⅔ cup
Snipped chives			

1 Put the vegetables in a saucepan with the stock and herbs. Bring to the boil, reduce the heat, part-cover and simmer gently for 15 minutes until the vegetables are soft.

2 Purée in a blender or food processor and return to the pan.

3 Add the cheese and milk and heat until the cheese melts.

4 Ladle into bowls and sprinkle with chives before serving.

PREPARATION TIME: 10 MINUTES

COOKING TIME: 25 MINUTES

CALORIES: LESS THAN 150

Salmon and Prawn Bisque

SERVES 6	METRIC	IMPERIAL	AMERICAN
Can of creamed sweetcorn (corn)	300 g	11 oz	1 medium
Chicken stock, made with 1 stock cube	450 ml	¾ pt	2 cups
Skimmed milk	150 ml	¼ pt	⅔ cup
Can of pink salmon, drained, skin and bones removed	200 g	7 oz	1 small
Peeled prawns (shrimp)	50 g	2 oz	2 oz
Brandy	15 ml	1 tbsp	1 tbsp
Low-fat double (heavy) cream	30 ml	2 tbsp	2 tbsp
Salt and freshly ground black pepper			
Chopped parsley	30 ml	2 tbsp	2 tbsp

1 Mix together all the ingredients except half the parsley in a saucepan. Heat gently, stirring occasionally, until piping hot.

2 Ladle into warmed bowls and sprinkle with the remaining parsley.

PREPARATION TIME: 5 MINUTES   COOKING TIME: 5 MINUTES

CALORIES: LESS THAN 150

Greek Egg and Lemon Soup

SERVES 6	METRIC	IMPERIAL	AMERICAN
Lamb stock, made with 3 stock cubes	1.2 litres	2 pts	5 cups
Long-grain rice	50 g	2 oz	¼ cup
Lemon	1	1	1
Eggs	2	2	2
Salt and freshly ground black pepper			

1 Put the stock in a saucepan and bring to the boil. Add the rice and simmer for 10 minutes or until the rice is tender.

2 Thinly pare the rind from the lemon and cut it into thin strips. Plunge the rind in boiling water and leave to stand for 5 minutes. Drain and reserve for garnish.

3 Squeeze the juice from the lemon into a bowl. Add the eggs and whisk thoroughly. Add 2 ladlefuls of the hot stock to the eggs and whisk again.

4 Remove the soup from the heat, stir in the egg mixture and season with salt and pepper. Do not reheat.

5 Ladle into warmed bowls and garnish each with a few strips of lemon rind.

PREPARATION TIME:
5 MINUTES,
PLUS 5 MINUTES
STANDING TIME

COOKING TIME:
5 MINUTES

CALORIES: LESS THAN 150

Dieter's Cabbage Soup

SERVES 4	METRIC	IMPERIAL	AMERICAN
Onion, finely chopped	1	1	1
Low-fat spread	15 g	½ oz	1 tbsp
Green cabbage, finely shredded	225 g	8 oz	8 oz
Chicken stock, made with 2 stock cubes	600 ml	1 pt	2½ cups
Bouquet garni sachet	1	1	1
Chopped parsley	15 ml	1 tbsp	1 tbsp
Salt and freshly ground black pepper			
Very low-fat crème fraîche	60 ml	4 tbsp	4 tbsp
Caraway seeds	5 ml	1 tsp	1 tsp

1 Fry (sauté) the onion in the low-fat spread for 3 minutes, stirring, until lightly golden.

2 Add the cabbage, stock and bouquet garni. Bring to the boil, reduce the heat, part-cover and simmer for 10 minutes.

3 Add the parsley and salt and pepper to taste and simmer for a further 5 minutes until the cabbage is really tender. Remove the bouquet garni.

4 Ladle into warmed soup bowls. Top each with 15 ml/1 tbsp of crème fraîche and sprinkle with a few of the caraway seeds. Serve straight away.

PREPARATION TIME:
5 MINUTES

COOKING TIME:
15 MINUTES

CALORIES: LESS THAN 50

Chilled Scandinavian Cucumber Soup

SERVES 4	METRIC	IMPERIAL	AMERICAN
Cucumber	1	1	1
Salt and freshly ground black pepper			
Dried dill (dill weed)	10 ml	2 tsp	2 tsp
Cider vinegar	30 ml	2 tbsp	2 tbsp
Very low-fat plain yoghurt	300 ml	½ pt	1¼ cups
Skimmed milk	300 ml	½ pt	1¼ cups

1 Cut four thin slices off the cucumber and reserve for garnish.

2 Grate the remainder into a large bowl and sprinkle with salt. Leave to stand for 10 minutes.

3 Squeeze out all the moisture and drain off.

4 Stir in the dill, vinegar, a little pepper and the yoghurt. Chill, if time.

5 Just before serving, stir in the milk, ladle into bowls and garnish each with a reserved cucumber slice.

PREPARATION TIME:
5 MINUTES,
PLUS 10 MINUTES
STANDING TIME

CALORIES: LESS THAN 100

Beetroot and Orange Cooler

SERVES 6	METRIC	IMPERIAL	AMERICAN
Small cooked beetroot (red beets), grated	4	4	4
Cold vegetable stock, made with 2 stock cubes	600 ml	1 pt	2½ cups
Lemon juice	15 ml	1 tbsp	1 tbsp
Small oranges	2	2	2
Very low-fat crème fraîche	300 ml	½ pt	1¼ cups
Freshly ground black pepper			
Snipped chives			

1 Mix the beetroot with the stock and lemon juice in a bowl.

2 Finely grate the rind and squeeze the juice from one orange and add to the beetroot mixture.

3 Remove all the rind and pith from the second orange and cut into six slices to use as garnish.

4 Stir the crème fraîche into the beetroot mixture. Season to taste with pepper, then chill thoroughly.

5 Ladle into soup bowls and serve garnished with the orange slices and a sprinkling of snipped chives.

PREPARATION TIME:
10 MINUTES

CALORIES: LESS THAN 100

Jellied Consommé with Mushrooms

SERVES 4	METRIC	IMPERIAL	AMERICAN
Button mushrooms, sliced	100 g	4 oz	4 oz
Water	300 ml	½ pt	1¼ cups
Lemon juice	5 ml	1 tsp	1 tsp
Powdered gelatine	15 ml	1 tbsp	1 tbsp
Can of condensed beef consommé	295 g	10½ oz	1 medium
Sherry	45 ml	3 tbsp	3 tbsp
A dash of soy sauce			
Very low-fat fromage frais	20 ml	4 tsp	4 tsp

1 Simmer the mushrooms in the water and lemon juice for 4 minutes until tender. Turn into a large bowl.

2 Blend 30 ml/2 tbsp of the hot mushroom liquid with the gelatine in a cup. Place the cup in a pan of hot water and heat gently, stirring, until the gelatine dissolves (or dissolve in the microwave briefly).

3 Stir into the mushrooms and liquid with the consommé, sherry and soy sauce.

4 Leave to cool, then chill until just set.

5 Stir to break up, spoon into soup bowls and garnish each with 5 ml/1 tsp of the fromage frais.

PREPARATION TIME:
5 MINUTES,
PLUS CHILLING TIME

COOKING TIME:
5 MINUTES

CALORIES: LESS THAN 100

Tuna Pâté

SERVES 6	METRIC	IMPERIAL	AMERICAN
Can of tuna in brine, drained	185 g	6½ oz	1 small
Very low-fat soft cheese	200 g	7 oz	scant 1 cup
Lemon juice	15 ml	1 tbsp	1 tbsp
Cayenne	1.5 ml	¼ tsp	¼ tsp
Chopped parsley	15 ml	1 tbsp	1 tbsp
Salt and freshly ground black pepper			
Mixed salad garnish			
Paprika			
Lemon wedges	6	6	6
To serve:			
Puffed wheat crispbread	12	12	12

1 Mash the tuna with the cheese in a bowl.

2 Beat in the lemon juice, cayenne and parsley, seasoning to taste with salt and pepper.

3 Spoon on to a sheet of greaseproof (waxed) paper in a sausage shape, then roll up and chill for at least 30 minutes.

4 Unwrap and cut into 12 slices. Arrange on six serving plates with a colourful mixed salad garnish.

5 Dust the pâté with paprika and add a lemon wedge to each plate. Serve with puffed wheat crispbread.

PREPARATION TIME:
10 MINUTES,
PLUS CHILLING TIME

CALORIES: LESS THAN 100

Carrot and Orange Pâté

SERVES 6	METRIC	IMPERIAL	AMERICAN
Walnut oil	15 ml	1 tbsp	1 tbsp
Onion, chopped	1	1	1
Carrots, thinly sliced	450 g	1 lb	1 lb
Clear honey	30 ml	2 tbsp	2 tbsp
Very low-fat plain yoghurt	200 ml	7 fl oz	scant 1 cup
Salt and freshly ground black pepper			
Grated rind and juice of 1 orange			
Large iceberg lettuce leaves	6	6	6
Oranges, segmented	2	2	2
Walnut halves	6	6	6

1 Heat the oil in a large saucepan and fry (sauté) the onion for 2 minutes, stirring.

2 Add the carrots and toss for 1 minute.

3 Add the honey and just enough water to cover the carrots. Bring to the boil, cover and cook gently for about 8 minutes or until the carrots are really tender.

4 Drain and mash thoroughly. Leave to cool.

5 When cold, mix with the yoghurt, salt, pepper, orange rind and just enough orange juice to add flavour.

6 Spoon the mixture on to lettuce leaves and garnish with orange segments and a walnut half on each.

PREPARATION TIME:
10 MINUTES,
PLUS COOLING TIME

COOKING TIME:
15 MINUTES

CALORIES: LESS THAN 150

Potted Stilton with Pears

SERVES 8	METRIC	IMPERIAL	AMERICAN
Ripe Stilton, crumbled	100 g	4 oz	1 cup
Low-fat spread	75 g	3 oz	⅓ cup
Ground mace	1.5 ml	¼ tsp	¼ tsp
English made mustard	1.5 ml	¼ tsp	¼ tsp
Port	30 ml	2 tbsp	2 tbsp
Ripe pears	4	4	4
Lemon juice			
Watercress sprigs			
To serve:			
Rye crispbreads	16	16	16

1 Mash the cheese with the low-fat spread in a bowl. Work in the mace, mustard and port.

2 Pack into a small pot and chill.

3 Core and slice the unpeeled pears and toss in lemon juice.

4 Arrange the pear slices attractively on eight serving plates and add a spoonful of the potted Stilton to one side of each.

5 Garnish with watercress and serve each with two rye crispbreads.

PREPARATION TIME:
15 MINUTES,
PLUS CHILLING TIME

CALORIES: LESS THAN 150

Crab and Cucumber Savoury

SERVES 6	METRIC	IMPERIAL	AMERICAN
Large cucumber, diced	1	1	1
Low-fat spread	40 g	1½ oz	3 tbsp
Button mushrooms, sliced	225 g	8 oz	8 oz
Plain (all-purpose) flour	10 ml	2 tsp	2 tsp
Fish stock, made with ½ stock cube	150 ml	¼ pt	⅔ cup
Dry sherry	15 ml	1 tbsp	1 tbsp
Low-fat single (light) cream	90 ml	6 tbsp	6 tbsp
Can of white crabmeat	170 g	6 oz	1 small
Salt and freshly ground black pepper			
Cress			

1 Boil the cucumber in lightly salted water for 3 minutes. Drain.

2 In the same pan, melt the low-fat spread and cook the mushrooms, stirring, for 2 minutes.

3 Add the cucumber, cover and cook over a gentle heat for 2 minutes.

4 Stir in the flour, remove from the heat and blend in the stock, sherry and cream. Return to the heat, bring to the boil and cook for 2 minutes, stirring.

5 Add the crabmeat and season to taste. Heat through.

6 Spoon into six individual serving dishes and garnish each with a little cress.

PREPARATION TIME:
10 MINUTES

COOKING TIME:
15 MINUTES

CALORIES: LESS THAN 150

Avocado Cream

SERVES 4	METRIC	IMPERIAL	AMERICAN
Powdered gelatine	*15 ml*	*1 tbsp*	*1 tbsp*
Cold water	*45 ml*	*3 tbsp*	*3 tbsp*
Vegetable stock, made with *½ stock cube*	*150 ml*	*¼ pt*	*⅔ cup*
Large ripe avocado	*1*	*1*	*1*
Lemon juice	*10 ml*	*2 tsp*	*2 tsp*
Low-calorie mayonnaise	*60 ml*	*4 tbsp*	*4 tbsp*
A dash of Worcestershire sauce			
A dash of Tabasco sauce			
Snipped chives	*30 ml*	*2 tbsp*	*2 tbsp*
Piece of cucumber, very thinly *sliced*	*5 cm*	*2 in*	*2 in*

1 Mix the gelatine with the cold water in a small bowl and leave to soften for a few minutes.

2 Stand the bowl in a pan of gently simmering water and stir until the gelatine dissolves completely (or dissolve in the microwave briefly).

3 Stir into the stock and leave to cool.

4 Halve the avocado, remove the stone (pit) and scoop the flesh into a bowl. Mash well with the lemon juice.

5 Beat in the mayonnaise and flavour to taste with the Worcestershire and Tabasco sauces. Stir in the chives.

6 Stir the cooled but not set stock into the avocado mixture.

7 Divide between four individual small dishes and chill until set.

8 Cover the top of each with overlapping slices of cucumber and serve cold.

PREPARATION TIME:
20 MINUTES

COOKING TIME:
5 MINUTES

CALORIES: LESS THAN 150

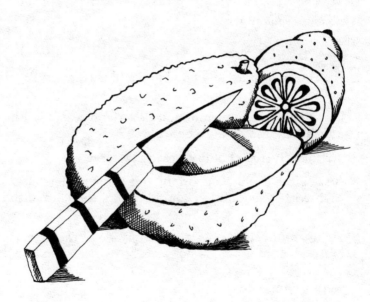

Artichoke and Prawn Cocktail

SERVES 6	METRIC	IMPERIAL	AMERICAN
Cans of artichoke hearts, drained and quartered	2×425 g	2×15 oz	2 large
Peeled prawns (shrimp)	225 g	8 oz	8 oz
Olive oil	45 ml	3 tbsp	3 tbsp
Lemon juice	30 ml	2 tbsp	2 tbsp
Salt and freshly ground black pepper			
Soured (dairy sour) cream	150 ml	¼ pt	⅔ cup
Jar of Danish lumpfish roe	50 g	2 oz	1 small
Whole unpeeled prawns	6	6	6

1 Put the artichokes in a bowl and add the peeled prawns.

2 Drizzle the oil and lemon juice over and season with a little salt and lots of pepper.

3 Toss gently and chill until ready to serve.

4 Just before serving, spoon into six wine goblets. Top each with a spoonful of soured cream, then lumpfish roe.

5 Hang an unpeeled prawn over the side of each glass and serve.

PREPARATION TIME:
10 MINUTES,
PLUS CHILLING TIME

CALORIES: LESS THAN 150

Normandy Tomatoes

SERVES 8	METRIC	IMPERIAL	AMERICAN
Green eating (dessert) apple	*1*	*1*	*1*
Lemon juice			
Large beefsteak tomatoes, halved	*8*	*8*	*8*
Camembert cheese, chopped	*225 g*	*8 oz*	*2 cups*
Fresh breadcrumbs	*50 g*	*2 oz*	*1 cup*
Kirsch or Calvados	*5 ml*	*1 tsp*	*1 tsp*
A little chopped parsley			
Watercress			

1 Core, halve and slice the apple and toss in lemon juice.

2 Scoop the seeds out of the tomatoes. Place the shells in a large shallow flameproof dish.

3 Mix the cheese with the breadcrumbs, Kirsch or Calvados and parsley. Spoon into the shells.

4 Place under a moderate grill (broiler) until the cheese melts and bubbles and the tomatoes are hot through. Reduce the heat to low, if necessary, so the tops do not become too brown.

5 Transfer to warmed plates and garnish with watercress and the apple slices.

PREPARATION TIME: COOKING TIME:
10 MINUTES 5 MINUTES

CALORIES: LESS THAN 150

Asparagus with Sun-dried Tomato Hollandaise

SERVES 4	METRIC	IMPERIAL	AMERICAN
Asparagus spears, trimmed	750 g	1½ lb	1½ lb
Egg yolks	2	2	2
Lemon juice	30 ml	2 tbsp	2 tbsp
Salt and freshly ground black pepper			
Paprika	5 ml	1 tsp	1 tsp
Low-fat spread	100 g	4 oz	½ cup
Sun-dried tomatoes, finely chopped	2	2	2
Chopped parsley	30 ml	2 tbsp	2 tbsp

1 Tie the asparagus spears in a bundle and stand in a saucepan of salted water. Bring to the boil, cover, reduce the heat to moderate and cook for 10 minutes. Turn off the heat and leave undisturbed for 5 minutes.

2 Meanwhile, put the egg yolks, lemon juice, salt, pepper and paprika in a small bowl over a pan of hot water. Whisk gently until the sauce starts to thicken.

3 Whisk in the low-fat spread a little at a time, whisking until thick and creamy.

4 Stir in the sun-dried tomatoes and parsley.

5 Lay the asparagus on warmed plates and spoon the sauce over, just below the tips.

PREPARATION TIME:
20 MINUTES

COOKING TIME:
15 MINUTES

CALORIES: LESS THAN 150

Baked Mozzarella with Tomatoes

SERVES 6	METRIC	IMPERIAL	AMERICAN
Beefsteak tomatoes, sliced	6	6	6
Mozzarella cheese, grated	100 g	4 oz	1 cup
Black olives, stoned (pitted) and sliced	6	6	6
Basil leaves, torn	12	12	12
Freshly ground black pepper			
Extra virgin olive oil	15 ml	1 tbsp	1 tbsp
A squeeze of lemon juice			
Slices of bread, diced	2	2	2
Garlic salt			

1 Lay the tomato slices overlapping in six individual shallow ovenproof dishes. Sprinkle with cheese, olives, basil, pepper, olive oil and lemon juice.

2 Place the diced bread on a baking sheet and sprinkle with garlic salt.

3 Put the bread on the top shelf of the oven and the tomato dishes on the next shelf.

4 Bake in a preheated oven at 200°C/400°F/gas mark 6 for about 8–10 minutes or until the bread is crisp and golden and the cheese has just melted.

5 Remove from the oven. Sprinkle the croûtons over the cheese and tomato and serve.

PREPARATION TIME: 20 MINUTES COOKING TIME: 10 MINUTES

CALORIES: LESS THAN 150

Greek Stuffed Aubergine

SERVES 6	METRIC	IMPERIAL	AMERICAN
Aubergines (eggplants)	3	3	3
Long-grain rice	40 g	1½ oz	3 tbsp
Minced (ground) lamb	175 g	6 oz	1½ cups
Onion, finely chopped	1	1	1
Garlic clove, crushed	1	1	1
Tomato purée (paste)	30 ml	2 tbsp	2 tbsp
Ground cinnamon	5 ml	1 tsp	1 tsp
Water	90 ml	6 tbsp	6 tbsp
Dried oregano	2.5 ml	½ tsp	½ tsp
Salt and freshly ground black pepper			
Low-fat Cheddar cheese, grated	40 g	1½ oz	⅓ cup

1 Halve the aubergines lengthways. Boil in a large flameproof casserole (Dutch oven) in lightly salted water until just tender. Drain, rinse with cold water and drain again.

2 Using a spoon, carefully scoop out the flesh, leaving a wall about 5 mm/¼ in thick. Chop the scooped-out flesh.

3 Cook the rice in boiling salted water until tender. Drain.

4 Dry-fry (sauté) the minced lamb in a saucepan until the fat runs. Pour off the fat.

5 Add the onion and continue frying for 2–3 minutes until all the grains of meat are separate and the onion is soft.

6 Add the chopped aubergine, rice and all the remaining ingredients except the cheese, seasoning to taste with salt and pepper.

7 Return the aubergine shells to the casserole in a single layer. Spoon the filling into the shells. Sprinkle the cheese on top.

8 Add enough boiling water to come half-way up the aubergine shells. Cover and simmer gently for 15 minutes.

9 Transfer to warmed plates and serve.

PREPARATION TIME: 15 MINUTES COOKING TIME: 45 MINUTES

CALORIES: LESS THAN 150

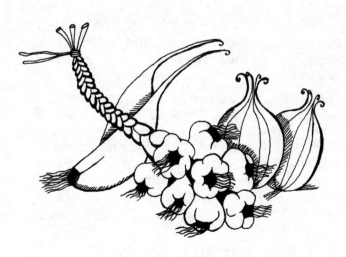

Simple Dolmas

SERVES 6	METRIC	IMPERIAL	AMERICAN
Large outer cabbage leaves	6	6	6
Frozen diced mixed vegetables	175 g	6 oz	6 oz
Dried oregano	2.5 ml	½ tsp	½ tsp
Salt and freshly ground black pepper			
Egg, beaten	1	1	1
Passata (sieved tomatoes)	250 ml	8 fl oz	1 cup
Grated low-fat Cheddar cheese	60 ml	4 tbsp	4 tbsp

1 Cut out and discard any thick central stalk from the leaves. Blanch in boiling water for 5 minutes. Drain and rinse with cold water.

2 Meanwhile, cook the vegetables according to the packet directions. Drain and mix with the oregano, a little salt and pepper and the beaten egg.

3 Lay the cabbage leaves on a board and divide the vegetable mixture between them. Fold in the two sides and roll up to form parcels.

4 Place, rolled sides down, in a single layer in an ovenproof dish. Spoon the passata over, sprinkle with the cheese and bake in a preheated oven at 190°C/375°F/gas mark 5 for 15–20 minutes until tender and the cheese has melted and is turning golden. Serve on warmed plates.

PREPARATION TIME:
5 MINUTES

COOKING TIME:
30 MINUTES

CALORIES: LESS THAN 150

LUNCHES, SUPPERS AND SNACKS

In this section you'll find some really

delicious ideas for lunch or supper. Serve

them on their own or with as much mixed

green salad as you wish, dressed with lemon

juice or wine vinegar, herbs, a dash of

Worcestershire sauce and black pepper. If you

can't resist salad cream, use just 5 ml/1 tsp

of low-calorie dressing. Don't forget that a

nectarine, an apple, a couple of plums

or a kiwi fruit make a tasty snack

at less than 50 calories.

Baked Potato Cakes with Caraway

MAKES 12	METRIC	IMPERIAL	AMERICAN
Cooked potato, well-mashed	450 g	1 lb	2 cups
Low-fat spread, plus extra for spreading	50 g	2 oz	¼ cup
Wholemeal flour	50 g	2 oz	½ cup
A pinch of salt			
Caraway seeds	30 ml	2 tbsp	2 tbsp

To serve:

1 thin slice of lean ham per portion

1 Beat the potato well, then beat in the low-fat spread, flour and salt.

2 Turn out on to a lightly floured surface and pat out to about 1 cm/½ in thick.

3 Cut into rounds using a 7.5 cm/3 in biscuit (cookie) cutter. Knead the trimmings together and cut again.

4 Place on a baking sheet and sprinkle with the caraway seeds, pressing them lightly into the surfaces.

5 Bake in a preheated oven at 200°C/400°F/gas mark 6 for about 20 minutes until lightly golden.

6 Serve two hot cakes per portion with a scraping of low-fat spread and a thin slice of lean ham.

PREPARATION TIME: 15 MINUTES

COOKING TIME: 20 MINUTES

CALORIES: LESS THAN 200

Russian Potatoes

SERVES 4	METRIC	IMPERIAL	AMERICAN
Large unpeeled potatoes	4	4	4
Can of diced mixed vegetables, drained	275 g	10 oz	1 medium
Low-calorie mayonnaise	30 ml	2 tbsp	2 tbsp
Chopped parsley	15 ml	1 tbsp	1 tbsp
Freshly ground black pepper			
Caraway seeds	5 ml	1 tsp	1 tsp

1 Scrub the potatoes and prick all over with a fork.

2 Bake in a preheated oven at 190°C/375°F/gas mark 5 for about 1 hour or until the potatoes feel soft when squeezed. Alternatively, cook in the microwave according to the manufacturer's instructions.

3 Meanwhile, mix the vegetables with the mayonnaise, parsley and pepper.

4 Cut a large cross in the top of each potato and squeeze the sides gently to open.

5 Spoon over the vegetable salad and sprinkle with caraway seeds before serving.

PREPARATION TIME:
5 MINUTES

COOKING TIME:
1 HOUR

CALORIES: LESS THAN 300

Mushrooms and Tomatoes in the Hole

SERVES 4	METRIC	IMPERIAL	AMERICAN
Button mushrooms	8	8	8
Tomatoes, halved	4	4	4
Sunflower oil	30 ml	2 tbsp	2 tbsp
Plain (all-purpose) flour	100 g	4 oz	1 cup
A pinch of salt			
Dried sage	5 ml	1 tsp	1 tsp
Eggs	2	2	2
Skimmed milk	150 ml	¼ pt	⅔ cup
Water	150 ml	¼ pt	⅔ cup

1 Arrange the mushrooms and tomatoes in a small roasting tin (pan).

2 Drizzle the oil over and place in a preheated oven at 220°C/425°F/gas mark 7 for 5 minutes.

3 Meanwhile, put the flour and salt in a bowl with the sage. Add the eggs and half the milk and water. Beat well until smooth.

4 Stir in the remaining milk and water.

5 Pour into the roasting tin and return to the oven for about 30 minutes until well risen, crisp and golden. Serve straight away.

PREPARATION TIME: 10 MINUTES

COOKING TIME: 35–40 MINUTES

CALORIES: LESS THAN 300

Oven Omelette Wedges

SERVES 4	METRIC	IMPERIAL	AMERICAN
Low-fat spread	5 ml	1 tsp	1 tsp
Eggs, beaten	4	4	4
Very low-fat cottage cheese	250 g	9 oz	generous 1 cup
Skimmed milk	150 ml	¼ pt	⅔ cup
Salt and freshly ground black pepper			
Button mushrooms, sliced	100 g	4 oz	4 oz
Onion, finely chopped	1	1	1
A pinch of dried mixed herbs			
Tomatoes, sliced	2	2	2
Parsley sprigs			

1 Lightly grease a shallow baking dish with the low-fat spread.

2 Mix together all the remaining ingredients except the tomatoes and parsley in a bowl and pour into the dish.

3 Bake in a preheated oven at 200°C/400°F/gas mark 6 for 20 minutes until golden brown and firm to the touch.

4 Serve cut into wedges, garnished with tomato slices and parsley sprigs.

PREPARATION TIME:
10 MINUTES

COOKING TIME:
20 MINUTES

CALORIES: LESS THAN 200

Cheese and Asparagus Soufflé

SERVES 4	METRIC	IMPERIAL	AMERICAN
Low-fat spread	5 ml	1 tsp	1 tsp
Can of cut asparagus, drained	295 g	10½ oz	1 medium
Can of condensed asparagus soup	295 g	10½ oz	1 medium
Parmesan cheese, grated	75 g	3 oz	¾ cup
Eggs, separated	4	4	4
Freshly ground black pepper			

1 Grease an 18 cm/7 in soufflé dish with the low-fat spread. Put the asparagus in the base.

2 Empty the soup into a bowl. Whisk in the cheese and egg yolks. Add pepper to taste.

3 Whisk the egg whites until stiff. Fold into the cheese mixture with a metal spoon.

4 Turn into the dish and bake in a preheated oven at 200°C/400°F/gas mark 6 for 25–30 minutes until well risen and golden brown.

5 Serve straight away.

PREPARATION TIME:
20 MINUTES

COOKING TIME:
25–30 MINUTES

CALORIES: LESS THAN 300

Leek and Apple Pockets

SERVES 2	METRIC	IMPERIAL	AMERICAN
Leeks, sliced	2	2	2
Vegetable stock, made with ½ stock cube	150 ml	¼ pt	⅔ cup
Large eating (dessert) apple	1	1	1
Shredded lettuce	30 ml	2 tbsp	2 tbsp
Small red (bell) pepper, chopped	½	½	½
Very low-fat cottage cheese	60 ml	4 tbsp	4 tbsp
Salt and freshly ground black pepper			
Pitta breads	2	2	2

1 Cook the leeks in the stock until tender. Drain (reserve the stock to add to soup). Leave to cool.

2 When cold, mix with the apple, lettuce, chopped pepper, cheese and seasoning to taste.

3 Grill (broil) or microwave the pitta breads briefly to puff them up. Make a slit along one edge to form a pocket.

4 Fill with the leek and apple mixture and serve straight away.

PREPARATION TIME: 10 MINUTES

COOKING TIME: 10 MINUTES

CALORIES: LESS THAN 300

Pear Extravaganza

SERVES 2	METRIC	IMPERIAL	AMERICAN
Wholemeal muffins	2	2	2
Low-fat spread	20 ml	4 tsp	4 tsp
Thin slices of lean Parma (or similar) ham	2	2	2
Pears, peeled, halved and cored	2	2	2
Basil leaves, shredded	6	6	6
Mozzarella cheese, grated	50 g	2 oz	½ cup
Freshly ground black pepper			
Small basil sprigs	2	2	2

1 Halve and toast the muffins, then spread with the low-fat spread.

2 Put half a slice of Parma ham on each muffin half. Place two halves on each of two flameproof plates.

3 Cut a thin slice off the rounded ends of the pears so they will stand up. Place them, cored sides up, on the muffin halves and put the pear slices in the core holes.

4 Sprinkle with the shredded basil leaves and top with the cheese. Add a good grinding of pepper.

5 Flash under a hot grill (broiler) until the cheese has melted.

6 Serve each garnished with a small basil sprig.

PREPARATION TIME: 15 MINUTES

COOKING TIME: 5 MINUTES

CALORIES: LESS THAN 300

Sardine Pyramids

SERVES 2	METRIC	IMPERIAL	AMERICAN
Crumpets	2	2	2
Low-fat spread	10 ml	2 tsp	2 tsp
Can of sardines in tomato sauce	120 g	4½ oz	1 small
Piece of cucumber, finely chopped	2.5 cm	1 in	1 in
Lemon juice			
Freshly ground black pepper			
Small lemon twists			

1 Toast the crumpets and spread with the low-fat spread.

2 Meanwhile, mash the sardines with their bones and mix with the cucumber and a squeeze of lemon juice. Season to taste with pepper.

3 Pile on to the crumpets and garnish each with a small lemon twist.

PREPARATION TIME: 5 MINUTES

COOKING TIME: 5 MINUTES

CALORIES: LESS THAN 300

French-style Ham and Eggs

SERVES 4	METRIC	IMPERIAL	AMERICAN
Onion, chopped	1	1	1
Low-fat spread	15 g	½ oz	1 tbsp
Button mushrooms, sliced	225 g	8 oz	8 oz
Garlic clove, crushed	1	1	1
Chicken stock, made with ½ stock cube	150 ml	¼ pt	⅔ cup
Lean cooked ham, diced	100 g	4 oz	1 cup
Chopped tarragon	10 ml	2 tsp	2 tsp
Chopped parsley	15 ml	1 tbsp	1 tbsp
Salt and freshly ground black pepper			
Eggs	4	4	4
Low-fat single (light) cream	30 ml	2 tbsp	2 tbsp
Thin slices of French stick	8	8	8

1 Fry (sauté) the onion in the low-fat spread in a large frying pan (skillet) for 3 minutes, stirring, until soft and lightly golden.

2 Add the mushrooms, garlic and stock. Bring to the boil and simmer for 5 minutes.

3 Add the ham, herbs and a little salt and pepper and continue cooking for 5 minutes.

4 Make four 'wells' in the mixture and break an egg into each. Drizzle the cream over.

5 Cover with foil or a lid and cook gently for 5 minutes or until the eggs are cooked to your liking.

6 Meanwhile, toast the French bread. Stand the toasted slices around the edge of the mixture, resting against the sides and serve straight from the pan.

PREPARATION TIME:
15 MINUTES

COOKING TIME:
20 MINUTES

CALORIES: LESS THAN 300

Rigatoni with Tomato and Basil Sauce

SERVES 4	METRIC	IMPERIAL	AMERICAN
Rigatoni	175 g	6 oz	6 oz
Passata (sieved tomatoes)	300 ml	½ pt	1¼ cups
Salt and freshly ground black pepper			
Chopped basil	15 ml	1 tbsp	1 tbsp
Grated Parmesan cheese	40 ml	8 tsp	8 tsp

1 Cook the rigatoni according to the packet directions. Drain and return to the pan.

2 Add the passata, a little salt, lots of pepper and the basil. Heat through, stirring gently.

3 Pile on to plates and sprinkle each with 10 ml/2 tsp of the cheese.

PREPARATION TIME:
10 MINUTES

COOKING TIME:
15 MINUTES

CALORIES: LESS THAN 200

Savoury Chicken Toasts

SERVES 4	METRIC	IMPERIAL	AMERICAN
Button mushrooms	75 g	3 oz	3 oz
Water	30 ml	2 tbsp	2 tbsp
Cornflour (cornstarch)	30 ml	2 tbsp	2 tbsp
Skimmed milk	250 ml	8 fl oz	1 cup
Low-fat spread	5 ml	1 tsp	1 tsp
Salt and freshly ground black pepper			
Chopped parsley	15 ml	1 tbsp	1 tbsp
Chopped thyme	15 ml	1 tbsp	1 tbsp
Cooked chicken, skin removed, chopped	175 g	6 oz	1½ cups
Slices of bread	4	4	4
Low-fat Cheddar cheese, grated	50 g	2 oz	½ cup
Parsley sprigs			

1 Stew the mushrooms in the water until tender. Boil rapidly to evaporate the liquid.

2 Blend the cornflour with a little of the milk, stir in the remaining milk and add to the pan with the low-fat spread.

3 Bring to the boil and cook for 2 minutes, stirring all the time until thick.

4 Season to taste and stir in the chopped herbs and chicken. Heat through.

5 Toast the bread on both sides under a hot grill (broiler). Spoon the chicken mixture on top and cover with the grated cheese.

6 Return to the grill until the cheese melts and bubbles. Serve straight away, garnished with parsley sprigs.

PREPARATION TIME:
10 MINUTES

COOKING TIME:
15 MINUTES

CALORIES: LESS THAN 300

Cheesy Beano

SERVES 2	METRIC	IMPERIAL	AMERICAN
Small slices of bread	2	2	2
Brown table sauce	10 ml	2 tsp	2 tsp
Can of no-added-sugar baked beans	400 g	14 oz	1 large
Low-fat Cheddar cheese, grated	30 ml	2 tbsp	2 tbsp

1 Toast the bread on both sides and spread one side with the sauce. Place on warmed flameproof plates.

2 Meanwhile, heat the beans in a saucepan. Spoon over the toast, sprinkle with the cheese and flash under a hot grill (broiler) until the cheese melts. Serve straight away.

PREPARATION TIME:
5 MINUTES

COOKING TIME:
5 MINUTES

CALORIES: LESS THAN 250

Cottage Griddle Cakes

MAKES 12	METRIC	IMPERIAL	AMERICAN
Low-fat spread, melted	25 g	1 oz	2 tbsp
Low-fat cottage cheese with chives	100 g	4 oz	½ cup
Eggs, beaten	2	2	2
Plain (all-purpose) flour	50 g	2 oz	½ cup
Baking powder	5 ml	1 tsp	1 tsp
Skimmed milk	15 ml	1 tbsp	1 tbsp

Low-fat spread, for greasing

To serve:

1 rasher (slice) grilled (broiled) lean back bacon per portion

1 Mix the melted low-fat spread with the cheese and beat in the eggs, flour, baking powder and milk to form a thick batter.

2 Heat a little low-fat spread in a heavy-based frying pan (skillet). Pour off any excess.

3 Drop spoonfuls of the batter into the pan and cook until the undersides are golden.

4 Flip over with a palette knife and cook the other side until brown.

5 Wrap in a clean napkin while cooking the remainder.

6 Serve two per person with a rasher of bacon. They can be reheated very briefly in the microwave or on a plate over a pan of hot water.

PREPARATION TIME:
5 MINUTES

COOKING TIME:
10 MINUTES

CALORIES: LESS THAN 200

Curried Beans on Toast

SERVES 2	METRIC	IMPERIAL	AMERICAN
Slices of bread	2	2	2
Low-fat spread	10 ml	2 tsp	2 tsp
Can of no-added-sugar baked beans	400 g	14 oz	1 large
Sultanas (golden raisins)	30 ml	2 tbsp	2 tbsp
Curry paste	5–10 ml	1–2 tsp	1–2 tsp
Chopped coriander (cilantro) leaves			

1 Toast the bread on both sides and spread with the low-fat spread.

2 Meanwhile, heat the beans in a saucepan with the sultanas and curry paste, stirring gently.

3 Spoon on to the bread and serve, sprinkled with a little chopped coriander.

PREPARATION TIME: 5 MINUTES

COOKING TIME: 5 MINUTES

CALORIES: LESS THAN 300

Bacon and Banana Grill

SERVES 1	METRIC	IMPERIAL	AMERICAN
Slices of bread	2	2	2
Low-fat spread	10 ml	2 tsp	2 tsp
Lean rashers (slices) streaky bacon, rinded	2	2	2
Small banana, mashed	1	1	1
A pinch of cayenne			

1 Spread one side of each bread slice with 5 ml/1 tsp low-fat spread. Put one slice, spread side down, on a board.

2 Grill (broil) the bacon until crisp.

3 Spread the mashed banana on the bread and crumble the bacon on top. Sprinkle with cayenne.

4 Top with the second slice, spread side up.

5 Grill or fry (sauté) until golden on both sides, pressing down with a fish slice during cooking. Serve cut into quarters.

PREPARATION TIME:
5 MINUTES

COOKING TIME:
10 MINUTES

CALORIES: LESS THAN 300

Mega Open Sandwiches

SERVES 1

- **Pastrami with Horseradish Spread:** mash 10 ml/ 2 tsp low-fat spread with 5 ml/1 tsp horseradish sauce. Spread on a slice of rye bread, then cut in half. Top each with a slice of pastrami. Top the pastrami with sliced radishes and a sprinkling of cress.

- **Pork and Apple Bounty:** spread a slice of wholemeal bread with a scraping of low-fat spread. Top with a thin slice of roast leg of pork, lean only. Cut in half. Top with slices of eating (dessert) apple dipped in lemon juice. Mix 10 ml/2 tsp low-calorie mayonnaise with two chopped sage leaves. Put a dollop on top of each open sandwich and garnish with a small fresh sage sprig.

- **Liver Sausage Lovely:** mash 10 ml/2 tsp low-fat spread with 15 ml/1 tbsp sweet pickle. Spread on a slice of bread, crusts removed. Cut in half. Top each with two thin slices of liver sausage, halved, and arrange overlapping on the bread. Top each with a cucumber twist.

- **Berlin Beauty:** spread a slice of pumpernickel very thinly with low-fat spread, then German mustard. Top with a thin slice of Emmental (Swiss) cheese, then a spoonful of drained sauerkraut. Sprinkle with caraway seeds.

- **Cheese and Walnut Whopper:** mix 15 ml/1 tbsp very low-fat soft cheese with 10 ml/2 tsp chopped walnuts. Spread on a slice of wholemeal bread and cut in half. Grate a chunk of cucumber and squeeze out the excess moisture. Add a dash of vinegar and toss with some freshly ground black pepper. Pile on the nutty cheese and garnish each with a walnut half.

CALORIES: LESS THAN 200

Savoury Satisfiers

SERVES 1

- 25 g/1 oz/2 tbsp extra-light very low-fat soft cheese, flavoured with snipped chives, and 2 carrots or celery sticks cut into matchsticks, to dunk

- 25 g/1 oz/2 tbsp virtually fat-free fromage frais, flavoured with 5 ml/1 tsp yeast extract and spread in celery sticks, then cut into short lengths

- 1 skinned and finely chopped tomato mixed with 25 g/1 oz/2 tbsp extra-light very low-fat soft cheese and a dash of Worcestershire and Tabasco sauces, with matchsticks of cucumber, celery and carrot to dip in

- 25 g/1 oz/2 tbsp extra-light very low-fat soft cheese, spread in celery sticks, sprinkled with fennel or caraway seeds and cut into short lengths

- A low-calorie crispbread, spread with a scraping of low-fat spread and Dijon mustard topped with 1 thin slice of lean ham from a packet

- 15 ml/1 tbsp extra-light very low-fat soft cheese on a low-calorie crispbread, topped with cucumber slices and a good grinding of black pepper

- 15 ml/1 tbsp extra-light very low-fat soft cheese mixed with a dash of hot pepper sauce, spread on a low-calorie crispbread and topped with a pile of grated carrot and a sprinkling of poppy seeds

- 1 thin slice of square ham from a packet, spread with 15 ml/1 tbsp extra-light very low-fat soft cheese and ½ satsuma, finely chopped, then rolled up

CALORIES: LESS THAN 50

SEAFOOD MAIN MEALS

Fish is a slimmer's friend. It's full of flavour, rich in nutrients and relatively low in calories. It is highly recommended by nutritionists as part of a healthy diet – Eskimos have one of the lowest incidences of heart disease in the world! Fish can also be exotic or everyday and is always quick to cook, so it should be a favourite with everyone.

Hot and Sour Cod

SERVES 4	METRIC	IMPERIAL	AMERICAN
Pieces of cod fillet, about 175 g/6 oz each	4	4	4
Low-fat spread	50 g	2 oz	¼ cup
Lemon juice	45 ml	3 tbsp	3 tbsp
Tabasco sauce	5 ml	1 tsp	1 tsp
Salt and freshly ground black pepper			
Spring onions (scallions), trimmed	8	8	8
Red (bell) peppers, quartered	2	2	2
Basmati rice, boiled	175 g	6 oz	¾ cup

To serve:

Chinese Leaf and Watercress Salad (see page 137)

1 Place the fish in a large, shallow dish.

2 Melt the low-fat spread with the lemon juice, Tabasco and salt and pepper and pour over the fish. Leave to marinate for 1 hour.

3 Transfer to a grill (broiler) rack. Add the spring onions and pepper quarters. Re-melt any remaining marinade and brush over.

4 Grill (broil) for about 5 minutes on each side until the vegetables are golden and the fish is cooked.

5 Serve hot with the rice and Chinese Leaf and Watercress Salad.

PREPARATION TIME:
10 MINUTES, PLUS
MARINATING TIME

COOKING TIME:
10 MINUTES

CALORIES: LESS THAN 350

Spicy Haddock with Beans

SERVES 4	METRIC	IMPERIAL	AMERICAN
Low-fat spread	25 g	1 oz	2 tbsp
Haddock fillet, skinned and cut into 4 pieces	750 g	1½ lb	1½ lb
Can of chopped tomatoes	228 g	8 oz	1 small
Tomato purée (paste)	15 ml	1 tbsp	1 tbsp
Can of cut green beans	275 g	10 oz	1 medium
Chilli powder	2.5 ml	½ tsp	½ tsp
A pinch of artificial sweetener			
Salt and freshly ground black pepper			
Long-grain rice, boiled	175 g	6 oz	¾ cup

1 Melt the low-fat spread in a large frying pan (skillet).

2 Fry (sauté) the fish for 5 minutes on one side. Turn over.

3 Add all the remaining ingredients except the rice and cover with foil or a lid.

4 Simmer for 5 minutes or until the fish is tender.

5 Serve on a bed of boiled rice.

PREPARATION TIME:
10 MINUTES

COOKING TIME:
15 MINUTES

CALORIES: LESS THAN 350

Plaice with Piquant Sauce

SERVES 4	METRIC	IMPERIAL	AMERICAN
Plaice fillets	4	4	4
Skimmed milk	250 ml	8 fl oz	1 cup
Water	250 ml	8 fl oz	1 cup
Low-fat spread	75 g	3 oz	⅓ cup
Grated rind and juice of 1 lemon			
Capers	45 ml	3 tbsp	3 tbsp
Salt and freshly ground black pepper			
A pinch of artificial sweetener			
Baby new potatoes, boiled	450 g	1 lb	1 lb
To serve:			
French (green) beans			

1 Skin the fillets if the skin is dark, then halve lengthways.

2 Roll them up and put in a single layer in a large flameproof casserole (Dutch oven).

3 Pour over the milk and water. Bring to the boil and simmer gently for about 7 minutes or until the fish is cooked but still holds its shape.

4 Meanwhile, melt the low-fat spread with the lemon rind and juice, capers, a little salt and pepper and sweeten to taste with sweetener.

5 Carefully transfer the fish to warmed plates, discarding the cooking liquid.

6 Spoon the piquant sauce over and serve with new
potatoes and French beans.

PREPARATION TIME:
10 MINUTES

COOKING TIME:
10 MINUTES

CALORIES: LESS THAN 350

Cheese and Garlic Haddock

SERVES 4	METRIC	IMPERIAL	AMERICAN
Low-fat spread	25 g	1 oz	2 tbsp
Pieces of haddock fillet, about 175 g/6 oz each	4	4	4
Low-fat Red Leicester cheese, grated	50 g	2 oz	½ cup
Skimmed milk	15 ml	1 tbsp	1 tbsp
Chopped parsley	15 ml	1 tbsp	1 tbsp
Small garlic clove, crushed	1	1	1
Salt and freshly ground black pepper			
Parsley sprigs			

To serve:

Dieter's Rosti (see page 129)

Tomatoes with Courgettes (see page 132)

1 Grease a shallow flameproof dish with a little of the low-fat spread. Put the fish in it, skinned sides up. Grill (broil) for 3 minutes. Turn over.

2 Mix the remaining low-fat spread with the cheese, milk, parsley, garlic and a little salt and pepper.

3 Spread over the fish and return to the grill (broiler) for about 10 minutes until golden and bubbling and the fish is cooked through.

4 Garnish with parsley sprigs and serve with Dieter's Rosti and Tomatoes with Courgettes.

PREPARATION TIME:
5 MINUTES

COOKING TIME:
15 MINUTES

CALORIES: LESS THAN 450

Fisherman's Crumble

SERVES 4	METRIC	IMPERIAL	AMERICAN
Plain (all-purpose) flour	75 g	3 oz	¾ cup
Paprika	10 ml	2 tsp	2 tsp
Low-fat spread	40 g	1½ oz	3 tbsp
Edam cheese, grated	50 g	2 oz	½ cup
White fish fillets, skinned and cubed	450 g	1 lb	1 lb
Can of condensed celery soup	295 g	10½ oz	1 medium
Frozen diced mixed vegetables	100 g	4 oz	4 oz
Dried mixed herbs	2.5 ml	½ tsp	½ tsp
Snipped chives	15 ml	1 tbsp	1 tbsp

To serve:

Broccoli

1 Put the flour in a bowl with the paprika.

2 Add the low-fat spread and rub in with the fingertips or a fork until the mixture resembles breadcrumbs.

3 Stir in the cheese.

4 Put the fish in an ovenproof dish and stir in the soup, vegetables and herbs.

5 Spoon the crumble mixture over and press down lightly. Bake in a preheated oven at 200°C/400°F/gas mark 6 for about 30 minutes until golden brown and cooked through.

6 Serve with broccoli.

PREPARATION TIME:
15 MINUTES

COOKING TIME:
30 MINUTES

CALORIES: LESS THAN 450

Peasant-style Swordfish

SERVES 4	METRIC	IMPERIAL	AMERICAN
Swordfish steaks, about 175 g/6 oz each	4	4	4
Extra virgin olive oil	5 ml	1 tsp	1 tsp
Low-fat spread	25 g	1 oz	2 tbsp
Garlic clove, chopped	1	1	1
Chopped parsley	30 ml	2 tbsp	2 tbsp
Salt and freshly ground black pepper			
Lemon wedges			
To serve:			
Baby new potatoes, scrubbed and boiled	450 g	1 lb	1 lb
Green salad			

1 Remove and discard the skin from the fish.

2 Fry (sauté) in the oil and low-fat spread for 5 minutes on one side until golden. Turn over.

3 Sprinkle with the garlic, parsley and salt and pepper.

4 Cover the pan with foil or a lid and cook gently for a further 5 minutes until cooked through and fragrant.

5 Arrange on warmed plates and spoon over the juices from the pan. Serve with lemon wedges, the potatoes and a green salad.

PREPARATION TIME:
10 MINUTES

COOKING TIME:
10 MINUTES

CALORIES: LESS THAN 350

Peppered Trout

SERVES 4	METRIC	IMPERIAL	AMERICAN
Low-fat spread	*25 g*	*1 oz*	*¼ cup*
Small rainbow trout, cleaned	*4*	*4*	*4*
Very low-fat soft cheese	*75 g*	*3 oz*	*⅓ cup*
Black peppercorns, coarsely crushed	*15 ml*	*1 tbsp*	*1 tbsp*
Skimmed milk	*45 ml*	*3 tbsp*	*3 tbsp*
Salt			
Chopped parsley			
To serve:			
Dieter's Rosti (see page 129)			
Broccoli			

1 Melt the low-fat spread in a large frying pan (skillet) and fry (sauté) the trout for about 5 minutes on each side until golden and cooked through. Transfer to warmed plates and keep warm.

2 Add the cheese to the juices in the pan with the peppercorns and a little of the milk.

3 Heat gently, stirring, until smooth. Thin with more milk until you have a smooth pouring consistency.

4 Season to taste with salt, then spoon over the trout and sprinkle with chopped parsley.

5 Serve with Dieter's Rosti and broccoli.

PREPARATION TIME:
15 MINUTES

COOKING TIME:
15 MINUTES

CALORIES: LESS THAN 350

Cod with Cheese and Anchovies

SERVES 4	METRIC	IMPERIAL	AMERICAN
Pieces of cod fillet, about 150 g/5 oz each, skinned	4	4	4
Low-fat spread	25 g	1 oz	2 tbsp
Ripe tomatoes, sliced	2	2	2
Mozzarella cheese, thinly sliced	100 g	4 oz	4 oz
Can of anchovies, drained	50 g	2 oz	1 small
A few torn basil leaves			
To serve:			
Small ciabatta loaf	1	1	1
Mixed salad			

1 Fry (sauté) the fish in the low-fat spread for 1 minute on each side.

2 Top with tomato slices, then the cheese.

3 Rinse the anchovy fillets and pat dry. Arrange attractively on top.

4 Cover the pan with foil or a lid and cook gently for about 6–7 minutes until the fish is cooked and the cheese has melted.

5 Transfer to warmed serving plates. Throw a few torn basil leaves over each and serve with the ciabatta loaf and a mixed salad.

PREPARATION TIME: 10 MINUTES

COOKING TIME: 10 MINUTES

CALORIES: LESS THAN 450

Prawn and Whiting Parcels

SERVES 4	METRIC	IMPERIAL	AMERICAN
Leeks, thinly sliced	4	4	4
Whiting fillets, about 175 g/6 oz each, skinned	4	4	4
Peeled prawns (shrimp)	100 g	4 oz	4 oz
Chopped dill (dill weed)	30 ml	2 tbsp	2 tbsp
Salt and freshly ground black pepper			
Juice of ½ lemon			
Capers	15 ml	1 tbsp	1 tbsp
Low-fat spread, melted	25 g	1 oz	2 tbsp
To serve:			
Small jacket-baked potatoes	4	4	4
French (green) beans			

1 Cut four large circles of baking parchment about 30 cm/12 in diameter. Fold in half, then open out.

2 Lay the sliced leeks over one half of each piece of parchment. Top with the whiting, then the prawns. Sprinkle with the dill, a little seasoning, the lemon juice and capers. Drizzle with the low-fat spread. Fold over the parchment and roll the edges to seal.

3 Transfer to a baking sheet. Bake in a preheated oven at 200°C/400°F/gas mark 6 for 25 minutes.

4 Serve with a small jacket-baked potato per portion and French beans.

PREPARATION TIME:
20 MINUTES

COOKING TIME:
25 MINUTES

CALORIES: LESS THAN 400

Prawn Supper

SERVES 4	METRIC	IMPERIAL	AMERICAN
Long-grain rice	100 g	4 oz	½ cup
Peeled prawns (shrimp)	225 g	8 oz	8 oz
Can of condensed cream of mushroom soup	295 g	10½ oz	1 medium
Low-fat Cheddar cheese, grated	50 g	2 oz	½ cup
Blue cheese, crumbled	25 g	1 oz	¼ cup
Reduced sugar and salt tomato ketchup (catsup)	10 ml	2 tsp	2 tsp
For the garnish:			
Celery stick	1	1	1
Piece of cucumber	5 cm	2 in	2 in
Carrot	1	1	1
Chopped parsley	15 ml	1 tbsp	1 tbsp
To serve:			
Garlic Bread (see page 135)			

1 Boil the rice according to the packet directions. Drain and mix with the remaining ingredients.

2 Spoon into an ovenproof dish and bake in a preheated oven at 180°C/350°F/gas mark 4 for about 30 minutes until piping hot.

3 Meanwhile, prepare the garnish. Cut the celery into three and cut each piece into very thin matchsticks. Cut the carrot into two or three pieces, then into very thin matchsticks. Mix together with the parsley.

4 Spoon the rice mixture on to warmed plates and garnish with a small pile of the celery mixture. Serve with Garlic Bread.

PREPARATION TIME:
15 MINUTES

COOKING TIME:
45 MINUTES

CALORIES: LESS THAN 450

Scallop, Mushroom and Courgette Kebabs

SERVES 4	METRIC	IMPERIAL	AMERICAN
Low-fat spread	40 g	1½ oz	3 tbsp
Onions, finely chopped	2	2	2
Can of chopped tomatoes	400 g	14 oz	1 large
Chopped basil	30 ml	2 tbsp	2 tbsp
Salt and freshly ground black pepper			
Courgettes (zucchini), cut into chunks	2	2	2
Small button mushrooms	100 g	4 oz	4 oz
Shelled scallops	350 g	12 oz	12 oz

To serve:

Crunchy-topped Tagliatelle (see page 131)

1 Melt 25 g/1 oz/2 tbsp of the low-fat spread in a saucepan. Add the onions and fry (sauté), stirring, for 2 minutes.

2 Add the tomatoes and simmer fairly rapidly for about 5 minutes until pulpy. Stir in the basil and season to taste.

3 Meanwhile, thread the courgettes, mushrooms and scallops on to soaked wooden skewers. Place on a grill (broiler) rack.

4 Melt the remaining low-fat spread and brush over.

5 Grill (broil) the kebabs, turning occasionally, for about 10 minutes, until cooked through and sizzling, brushing with any remaining low-fat spread during cooking.

6 Transfer to warmed plates and serve with the hot sauce and Crunchy-topped Tagliatelle.

<table>
<tr><td>PREPARATION TIME:
15 MINUTES</td><td></td><td>COOKING TIME:
20 MINUTES</td></tr>
</table>

CALORIES: LESS THAN 350

Midweek Paella

SERVES 4	METRIC	IMPERIAL	AMERICAN
Packet of savoury vegetable rice	*1*	*1*	*1*
Boiling water	*450 ml*	*¾ pt*	*2 cups*
Cooked chicken, diced	*100 g*	*4 oz*	*1 cup*
Can of mussels in brine, drained	*250 g*	*9 oz*	*1 medium*
Peeled prawns (shrimp)	*100 g*	*4 oz*	*4 oz*
Chopped parsley			

To serve:

Walnut Bread (see page 135)
Mixed green salad

1 Put the rice in a pan with the boiling water. Stir, cover and simmer for 12 minutes.

2 Add the remaining ingredients except the parsley and cook for a further 8 minutes until all the liquid has been absorbed and the rice is tender.

3 Spoon on to warmed plates, sprinkle with parsley and serve with Walnut Bread and a green salad.

<table>
<tr><td>PREPARATION TIME:
5 MINUTES</td><td></td><td>COOKING TIME:
20 MINUTES</td></tr>
</table>

CALORIES: LESS THAN 450

Seafood and Fennel Shells

SERVES 4	METRIC	IMPERIAL	AMERICAN
Multi-coloured pasta shells	225 g	8 oz	8 oz
Low-fat spread	25 g	1 oz	2 tbsp
Fennel bulb, finely chopped and green fronds reserved	1	1	1
Bunch of spring onions (scallions), chopped	1	1	1
Dry white wine	30 ml	2 tbsp	2 tbsp
Frozen seafood cocktail, thawed	225 g	8 oz	8 oz
Salt and freshly ground black pepper			
Chopped parsley	15 ml	1 tbsp	1 tbsp
Lemon wedges	4	4	4
To serve:			
Mixed leaf salad			

1 Cook the pasta according to the packet directions. Drain.

2 Meanwhile, melt the low-fat spread in a saucepan. Add the chopped fennel and spring onions and fry (sauté) for 3 minutes, stirring.

3 Cover with a lid, reduce the heat and cook for a further 5 minutes until tender.

4 Add the wine and seafood. Heat through, stirring gently, for about 3 minutes until piping hot.

5 Season to taste and add the parsley. Add the pasta shells and toss gently.

6 Pile on to warmed plates and garnish each with a lemon wedge and fennel frond. Serve with a mixed leaf salad.

PREPARATION TIME:
5 MINUTES

COOKING TIME:
15 MINUTES

CALORIES: LESS THAN 350

Swiss Fish Potato Cake

SERVES 4	METRIC	IMPERIAL	AMERICAN
Low-fat spread	25 g	1 oz	2 tbsp
Potatoes, grated	450 g	1 lb	1 lb
Salt and freshly ground black pepper			
White fish fillets, skinned and cut into small pieces	450 g	1 lb	1 lb
Grated rind of ½ lemon			
Chopped parsley	15 ml	1 tbsp	1 tbsp
Passata (sieved tomatoes)	300 ml	½ pt	1¼ cups
Chopped basil	5 ml	1 tsp	1 tsp
Lemon wedges			

To serve:

Mangetout (snow peas)

1 Melt the low-fat spread in a frying pan (skillet). Add half the potatoes and press down well. Season with salt and pepper.

2 Add the fish in an even layer and sprinkle with the lemon rind, parsley and a little seasoning.

3 Top with the remaining potatoes, press down well again and season lightly.

4 Cover with foil or a lid and cook gently for 30 minutes until cooked through.

5 Meanwhile, heat the passata with the basil in a small saucepan.

6 Turn the fish cake out on to a warmed serving plate. Garnish with lemon wedges and serve, cut into quarters, with the tomato sauce and mangetout.

PREPARATION TIME: 15 MINUTES COOKING TIME: 35 MINUTES

CALORIES: LESS THAN 450

Smoked Salmon and Broccoli Pappardelle

SERVES 4	METRIC	IMPERIAL	AMERICAN
Pappardelle (wide ribbon noodles)	225 g	8 oz	8 oz
Broccoli, cut into tiny florets	175 g	6 oz	6 oz
Smoked salmon pieces, cut up if necessary	100 g	4 oz	4 oz
Very low-fat quark	50 g	2 oz	¼ cup
Eggs	2	2	2
Skimmed milk	60 ml	4 tbsp	4 tbsp
Salt and freshly ground black pepper			
A squeeze of lemon juice			
Fresh Parmesan cheese, thinly shaved with a potato peeler	25 g	1 oz	1 oz

1 Cook the pasta according to the packet directions. Add the broccoli for the last 5 minutes cooking time.

2 Drain and return to the saucepan. Add the salmon and quark. Toss gently.

3 Beat together the eggs and milk and add to the pan with some salt and pepper.

4 Cook gently until creamy but not totally scrambled.

5 Taste and add lemon juice and seasoning if necessary.

6 Pile on to warmed plates and top with Parmesan.

PREPARATION TIME: 5 MINUTES

COOKING TIME: 20 MINUTES

CALORIES: LESS THAN 450

MEAT MAIN MEALS

Meat eaters can breathe a sigh of relief – you can still enjoy a steak or curry on this diet! But remember, always trim off all excess fat, choose extra-lean mince and remove any fat floating on a sauce after cooking. You can do this by laying kitchen paper (paper towels) on the surface, then carefully removing them when they have absorbed the fat; or you can allow the stew or casserole to go completely cold, skim off any fat, then reheat the dish until piping hot. Alternatively, try holding an ice cube and slowly drawing it across the surface; any fat will harden on the surface of the cube (you'll need two or three cubes).

Peppered Steak Madeira

SERVES 4	METRIC	IMPERIAL	AMERICAN
Small fillet steaks, about 150 g/5 oz each	4	4	4
Multi-coloured peppercorns, crushed	15 ml	1 tbsp	1 tbsp
Low-fat spread	25 g	1 oz	2 tbsp
Bunch of spring onions (scallions), finely chopped	1	1	1
Madeira	90 ml	6 tbsp	6 tbsp
Salt and freshly ground black pepper			
Parsley sprigs			
To serve:			
Nutty Wild Rice Mix (see page 133)			

1 Wipe the steaks and press the peppercorns into the surfaces.

2 Melt the low-fat spread and fry (sauté) the steaks for 4–6 minutes or until cooked to your liking. Lift them out of the pan and keep warm on warmed plates.

3 Add the spring onions to the pan and cook for 3 minutes, stirring.

4 Add the Madeira and cook until bubbling.

5 Season to taste and spoon over the steaks.

6 Garnish with parsley sprigs and serve with Nutty Wild Rice Mix.

PREPARATION TIME: 10 MINUTES

COOKING TIME: 15 MINUTES

CALORIES: LESS THAN 350

Beef Pasta Grill

SERVES 4	METRIC	IMPERIAL	AMERICAN
Pasta shapes	175 g	6 oz	6 oz
Onion, chopped	1	1	1
Very lean minced (ground) beef	225 g	8 oz	2 cups
Can of tomatoes	400 g	14 oz	1 large
Dried oregano	2.5 ml	½ tsp	½ tsp
Salt and freshly ground black pepper			
Grated low-fat Cheddar cheese	45 ml	3 tbsp	3 tbsp
To serve:			
Mixed green salad			

❀

1 Cook the pasta according to the packet directions. Drain.

2 Meanwhile, fry (sauté) the onion and beef together in a pan until the grains of meat are brown and separate. Pour off any fat.

3 Add the tomatoes and break up with a wooden spoon. Stir in the oregano and a little salt and pepper.

4 Bring to the boil, reduce the heat and simmer for 10 minutes.

5 Stir in the pasta.

6 Spoon into a flameproof dish. Top with the cheese and flash under a hot grill (broiler) to brown the top.

7 Serve with a mixed green salad.

PREPARATION TIME:
5 MINUTES

COOKING TIME:
30 MINUTES

CALORIES: LESS THAN 300

Corned Beef Hash

SERVES 4	METRIC	IMPERIAL	AMERICAN
Potatoes, diced	450 g	1 lb	1 lb
Can of corned beef	350 g	12 oz	1 medium
Onions, chopped	2	2	2
Low-fat spread	25 g	1 oz	2 tbsp
Can of no-added-sugar baked beans	400 g	14 oz	1 large
Worcestershire sauce	15 ml	1 tbsp	1 tbsp
Salt and freshly ground black pepper			
To serve:			
Mixed salad			
Hard-boiled (hard-cooked) eggs, quartered	4	4	4

1 Boil the potatoes in lightly salted water until tender. Drain.

2 Meanwhile, dice the corned beef, discarding any excess fat.

3 Melt the low-fat spread in a large frying pan (skillet) and fry (sauté) the onions for 3 minutes until soft but not brown.

4 Add the remaining ingredients, the potatoes and corned beef and fry, turning occasionally, for 5 minutes.

5 Press down the mixture with a fish slice and continue cooking for about 5 minutes until golden brown underneath.

6 Flash under a hot grill (broiler) to brown the top. Loosen and turn out on to a warmed plate.

7 Serve cut into quarters with a mixed salad garnished with the egg quarters.

PREPARATION TIME:
10 MINUTES

COOKING TIME:
15 MINUTES

CALORIES: LESS THAN 550

Lamb, Corn and Sun-dried Tomato Kebabs

SERVES 4	METRIC	IMPERIAL	AMERICAN
Lamb neck fillet, trimmed of any fat and sinews	350 g	12 oz	12 oz
Olive oil	15 ml	1 tbsp	1 tbsp
Lemon juice	15 ml	1 tbsp	1 tbsp
Dried oregano	2.5 ml	½ tsp	½ tsp
Dried mint	2.5 ml	½ tsp	½ tsp
Garlic clove, crushed	1	1	1
Salt and freshly ground black pepper			
Corn cobs, each cut into 6 pieces	2	2	2
Jar of sun-dried tomatoes, drained	285 g	10¼ oz	10¼ oz

To serve:

Tomatoes with Courgettes (see page 132)

Nutty Wild Rice Mix (see page 133)

Mixed leaf salad

1 Cut the meat into neat cubes and place in a shallow bowl.

2 Drizzle with the oil and lemon juice, and sprinkle with the oregano, mint, garlic and a little salt and pepper. Toss well and leave to marinate for at least 1 hour.

3 Plunge the corn cobs into boiling water for 3 minutes to soften slightly. Drain.

4 Thread the meat, corn and sun-dried tomatoes on eight skewers. Brush with any remaining marinade.

5 Place on a grill (broiler) rack. Grill (broil) for about 10 minutes, turning once or twice and brushing with any leftover marinade during cooking.

6 Transfer to warmed plates and serve with Tomatoes with Courgettes, Nutty Wild Rice Mix and a mixed leaf salad.

PREPARATION TIME:
10 MINUTES,
PLUS MARINATING TIME

COOKING TIME:
15 MINUTES

CALORIES: LESS THAN 450

Rich Savoury Lamb Steaks

SERVES 4	METRIC	IMPERIAL	AMERICAN
Lamb leg steaks, all fat removed	4	4	4
Plain (all-purpose) flour	30 ml	2 tbsp	2 tbsp
Salt and freshly ground black pepper			
Low-fat spread	25 g	1 oz	2 tbsp
Leeks, sliced	3	3	3
Can of condensed tomato soup	295 g	10½ oz	1 medium
Dried basil	5 ml	1 tsp	1 tsp
To serve:			
Rigatoni or other pasta, boiled	225 g	8 oz	8 oz
Parmesan cheese, grated	30 ml	2 tbsp	2 tbsp
Green salad			

1 Toss the lamb in seasoned flour.

2 Melt the low-fat spread in a flameproof casserole (Dutch oven) and fry (sauté) the leeks for 2 minutes until softened and lightly browned.

3 Add the lamb and brown on both sides. Pour off any excess fat.

4 Add the soup, basil and more salt and pepper.

5 Cover and cook in a preheated oven at 160°C/325°F/ gas mark 3 for 1½ hours.

6 Serve with the pasta sprinkled with the Parmesan cheese and a green salad.

PREPARATION TIME:
5 MINUTES

COOKING TIME:
1¾ HOURS

CALORIES: LESS THAN 450

Grilled Steak with Peppers

SERVES 4	METRIC	IMPERIAL	AMERICAN
Low-fat spread	15 g	½ oz	1 tbsp
Garlic clove, crushed	1	1	1
Chopped parsley	15 ml	1 tbsp	1 tbsp
Chopped basil	15 ml	1 tbsp	1 tbsp
Lemon juice	15 ml	1 tbsp	1 tbsp
Salt and freshly ground black pepper			
Thin fillet steaks, about 100 g/4 oz each	4	4	4
Red, green, yellow and orange (bell) peppers, cut into sixths	1 each	1 each	1 each

To serve:

Dieter's Rosti (see page 129)

Mixed salad

1 Melt the low-fat spread and stir in the garlic, herbs, lemon juice and a little salt and pepper.

2 Lay the steaks and peppers on a grill (broiler) rack. Brush all over with the garlic mixture.

3 Grill (broil), brushing and turning once, until the steaks and peppers are cooked through. If you like your steak rare, remove after about 4 minutes of cooking and keep warm while continuing to cook the peppers.

4 Transfer to warmed plates and serve with Dieter's Rosti and a mixed salad.

PREPARATION TIME: 10 MINUTES

COOKING TIME: 10–15 MINUTES

CALORIES: LESS THAN 450

Eastern Yoghurt Lamb

SERVES 4	METRIC	IMPERIAL	AMERICAN
Onion, sliced	1	1	1
Low-fat spread	15 g	½ oz	1 tbsp
Lean cooked lamb, diced	225 g	8 oz	2 cups
Garlic clove, crushed	1	1	1
Fresh root ginger, grated	2.5 ml	½ tsp	½ tsp
Ground cumin	2.5 ml	½ tsp	½ tsp
Ground coriander (cilantro)	2.5 ml	½ tsp	½ tsp
Turmeric	7.5 ml	1½ tsp	1½ tsp
Very low-fat plain yoghurt	150 ml	¼ pt	⅔ cup
Salt and freshly ground black pepper			
Packet of pilau rice	1	1	1
Desiccated (shredded) coconut	20 ml	4 tsp	4 tsp
Currants	30 ml	2 tbsp	2 tbsp

1 Fry (sauté) the onion in the low-fat spread until turning golden.

2 Add the lamb and all the remaining ingredients except the rice, coconut and currants.

3 Bring to the boil, reduce the heat and simmer for about 20 minutes. The mixture will curdle during cooking.

4 Meanwhile, cook the rice according to the packet directions. Pile on to four warmed plates.

5 Top with the lamb mixture and sprinkle with the coconut and currants before serving.

PREPARATION TIME:
5 MINUTES

COOKING TIME:
30 MINUTES

CALORIES: LESS THAN 350

Fragrant Lamb Cutlets

SERVES 4	METRIC	IMPERIAL	AMERICAN
Low-fat spread	25 g	1 oz	2 tbsp
Thin lamb cutlets, trimmed of fat	8	8	8
Garlic clove, finely chopped	1	1	1
Large rosemary sprig	1	1	1
Water	60 ml	4 tbsp	4 tbsp
Salt and freshly ground black pepper			
Small rosemary sprigs			

To serve:

Greek Village Salad (see page 136)

1 Melt the low-fat spread and brown the cutlets on both sides. Remove from the pan.

2 Spoon off any fat, leaving the juices. Add all the remaining ingredients except the small rosemary sprigs, return the cutlets, cover and cook gently for 10 minutes until the lamb is really tender.

3 Transfer to warmed serving plates, discarding the large rosemary sprig.

4 Taste and re-season the juices, if necessary. Pour over.

5 Garnish with rosemary and serve with Greek Village Salad.

PREPARATION TIME: 5 MINUTES

COOKING TIME: 20 MINUTES

CALORIES: LESS THAN 350

Brittany Lamb

SERVES 4	METRIC	IMPERIAL	AMERICAN
Onion, thinly sliced	1	1	1
Cooking (tart) apple, thinly sliced	1	1	1
Low-fat spread	15 g	½ oz	1 tbsp
Lamb chump chops, trimmed of fat	4	4	4
Cider or apple juice	300 ml	½ pt	1¼ cups
Chopped mint	15 ml	1 tbsp	1 tbsp
Salt and freshly ground black pepper			
Chopped parsley	15 ml	1 tbsp	1 tbsp

To serve:

Dieter's Rosti (see page 129)

French (green) beans

1 Fry (sauté) the onion and apple in the low-fat spread
  for 4 minutes until softened and lightly golden.
  Remove from the pan with a draining spoon and
  keep warm.

2 Add the chops and fry for 10–15 minutes until
  cooked to your liking, turning once.

3 Remove from the pan and add to the onion and
  apple. Spoon off all the fat, leaving the juices.

4 Add the cider or apple juice and the mint. Bring to
  the boil and boil rapidly until reduced by half. Season
  to taste.

5 Arrange the chops on four warmed serving plates
  and top with the onion and apple mixture.

6 Spoon the sauce over and sprinkle with the chopped parsley. Serve with Dieter's Rosti and French beans.

PREPARATION TIME:
10 MINUTES

COOKING TIME:
25–30 MINUTES

CALORIES: LESS THAN 350

Leftover Lamb Biryani

SERVES 4	METRIC	IMPERIAL	AMERICAN
Basmati rice, thoroughly rinsed	175 g	6 oz	¾ cup
Low-fat spread	25 g	1 oz	2 tbsp
Onions, thinly sliced	2	2	2
Curry paste	10 ml	2 tsp	2 tsp
Water	30 ml	2 tbsp	2 tbsp
Cooked lamb, diced	100 g	4 oz	1 cup
Ground coriander (cilantro)	2.5 ml	½ tsp	½ tsp
Ground cumin	2.5 ml	½ tsp	½ tsp
Tomato, finely chopped	1	1	1
Salt and freshly ground black pepper			
Sultanas (golden raisins)	30 ml	2 tbsp	2 tbsp
Chopped coriander leaves	45 ml	3 tbsp	3 tbsp
Desiccated (shredded) coconut	15 ml	1 tbsp	1 tbsp
Lettuce leaves, tomato wedges, cucumber slices, lemon wedges			

❀

1 Cook the rice according to the packet directions. Drain, rinse with cold water and drain again.

2 Melt the low-fat spread in a saucepan and fry (sauté) the onions until golden brown.

3 Stir in the curry paste, water, lamb, ground spices, tomato and a little salt and pepper. Stir-fry for about 5 minutes.

4 Add the sultanas, rice and coriander leaves, mix well and heat through.

5 Spoon on to four warmed plates, sprinkle with the coconut and serve garnished with lettuce, tomato, cucumber and lemon wedges.

PREPARATION TIME:
15 MINUTES

COOKING TIME:
15 MINUTES

CALORIES: LESS THAN 350

Frankfurter Supper

SERVES 4	METRIC	IMPERIAL	AMERICAN
Potatoes, cut into even-sized pieces	450 g	1 lb	1 lb
Jar of sauerkraut	550 g	1¼ lb	1 large
Caraway seeds	15 ml	1 tbsp	1 tbsp
Frankfurters or hot-dog sausages	16	16	16
Chopped parsley			
German mustard			

1 Cook the potatoes in boiling, lightly salted water until tender but still holding their shape. Drain.

2 Meanwhile, heat the sauerkraut in a saucepan with the caraway seeds.

3 Heat the frankfurters in a separate pan.

4 Spoon the sauerkraut on to four warmed plates with the frankfurters and potatoes.

5 Garnish with chopped parsley and serve with German mustard.

PREPARATION TIME:
5 MINUTES

COOKING TIME:
15 MINUTES

CALORIES: LESS THAN 350

Peppered Liver Deluxe

SERVES 4	METRIC	IMPERIAL	AMERICAN
Plain (all-purpose) flour	15 ml	1 tbsp	1 tbsp
Multi-coloured peppercorns, coarsely crushed	30 ml	2 tbsp	2 tbsp
Lambs' liver, very thinly sliced	225 g	8 oz	8 oz
Low-fat spread	25 g	1 oz	2 tbsp
Lemon juice	15 ml	1 tbsp	1 tbsp
Small onion, grated	1	1	1
Chopped parsley	30 ml	2 tbsp	2 tbsp
Worcestershire sauce	45 ml	3 tbsp	3 tbsp
Potatoes, boiled and mashed with a little skimmed milk	450 g	1 lb	1 lb
To serve:			
Carrots			

1 Mix the flour with the peppercorns and use to coat the liver slices.

2 Melt the low-fat spread in a large frying pan (skillet) and fry (sauté) the liver on one side until golden. Turn over and cook until the pink juices rise to the surface. Transfer to warmed serving plates.

3 Add the remaining ingredients to the juices in the pan and cook, stirring, for 1 minute.

4 Spoon over the liver and serve with the mashed potatoes and carrots.

PREPARATION TIME: 10 MINUTES

COOKING TIME: 10 MINUTES

CALORIES: LESS THAN 350

Barbecued Pork and Beans

SERVES 4	METRIC	IMPERIAL	AMERICAN
Onions, thinly sliced	2	2	2
Pork fillet, cubed	225 g	8 oz	8 oz
Low-fat spread	15 g	½ oz	1 tbsp
Cans of no-added-sugar baked beans	2×400 g	2×14 oz	2 large
Bottled barbecue sauce	30 ml	2 tbsp	2 tbsp
Slices of French stick	4	4	4
Wholegrain mustard	10 ml	2 tsp	2 tsp
Chopped parsley			
To serve:			
Mixed green salad			

1 Fry (sauté) the onions and pork in the low-fat spread in a saucepan for about 8 minutes until cooked through and golden. Pour off any fat.

2 Stir in the beans and barbecue sauce and heat through.

3 Meanwhile, toast the French bread and spread with the mustard.

4 Ladle the pork and beans into warmed soup bowls. Top each with a slice of French stick and sprinkle with chopped parsley.

5 Serve with a mixed green salad.

PREPARATION TIME: 10 MINUTES COOKING TIME: 10 MINUTES

CALORIES: LESS THAN 350

Glazed Nutty Pork

SERVES 4	METRIC	IMPERIAL	AMERICAN
Lean pork chops, trimmed of any fat	4	4	4
English made mustard	10 ml	2 tsp	2 tsp
Clear honey	15 ml	1 tbsp	1 tbsp
Raw peanuts, chopped	15 ml	1 tbsp	1 tbsp
Worcestershire sauce	5 ml	1 tsp	1 tsp
Salt	2.5 ml	½ tsp	½ tsp
Freshly ground black pepper			
Melted low-fat spread	5 ml	1 tsp	1 tsp

To serve:

Courgettes (zucchini) and carrots

1 Grill (broil) the chops for 5 minutes on each side until nearly cooked.

2 Mix together the remaining ingredients and spread over the chops.

3 Grill until golden brown and bubbling.

4 Transfer to warmed plates and serve with courgettes and carrots.

PREPARATION TIME:
10 MINUTES

COOKING TIME:
15 MINUTES

CALORIES: LESS THAN 450

Sage and Cheese Pork Fillets

SERVES 4	METRIC	IMPERIAL	AMERICAN
Pieces of pork fillet, about 100 g/4 oz each	4	4	4
Melted low-fat spread	10 ml	2 tsp	2 tsp
Sage leaves, chopped	8	8	8
Salt and freshly ground black pepper			
Gruyère or Emmental (Swiss) cheese, grated	50 g	2 oz	½ cup
New potatoes, boiled	450 g	1 lb	1 lb

To serve:

Green Beans with Cherry Tomatoes (see page 138)

1 Put the pork pieces in a plastic bag one at a time and beat flat with a rolling pin or meat mallet.

2 Place on a grill (broiler) rack and brush with half the low-fat spread.

3 Grill (broil) for about 4 minutes until golden. Turn over and brush with the remaining spread and grill for a further 4 minutes until cooked through.

4 Sprinkle with the chopped sage, a little salt and pepper, then the cheese and return to the grill until the cheese melts and bubbles. Serve with the potatoes and Green Beans with Cherry Tomatoes.

PREPARATION TIME:
10 MINUTES

COOKING TIME:
15 MINUTES

CALORIES: LESS THAN 450

Speedy Cassoulet

SERVES 4	METRIC	IMPERIAL	AMERICAN
Chipolata sausages, cut into chunks	4	4	4
Lean rashers (slices) streaky bacon, rinded and diced	2	2	2
Can of red kidney beans, drained	425 g	15 oz	1 large
Can of no-added-sugar baked beans	400 g	14 oz	1 large
Can of chopped tomatoes	400 g	14 oz	1 large
Worcestershire sauce			
Salt and freshly ground black pepper			
Chopped parsley			
To serve:			
Garlic Bread (see page 135)			

1 Dry-fry (sauté) the sausages and bacon in a saucepan until well browned and crisp.

2 Remove from the pan and drain on kitchen paper (paper towels). Wipe out the pan.

3 Add all the remaining ingredients except the parsley, seasoning to taste with Worcestershire sauce, salt and pepper. Heat through, stirring.

4 Add the sausages and bacon and heat through.

5 Spoon into bowls and sprinkle with parsley before serving with Garlic Bread.

PREPARATION TIME:
10 MINUTES

COOKING TIME:
20 MINUTES

CALORIES: LESS THAN 550

POULTRY MAIN MEALS

Chicken and turkey are ideal for slimmers.
They are naturally lower in fat than other
meats and, with the skin removed, are very
low indeed. Always make sure the meat is
cooked through, but don't overcook – turkey
steaks, in particular, can become very dry.

Orchard Chicken

SERVES 4	METRIC	IMPERIAL	AMERICAN
Small onion, finely chopped	1	1	1
Garlic clove, crushed	1	1	1
Artificial sweetener granules	1.5 ml	¼ tsp	¼ tsp
Dijon mustard	15 ml	1 tbsp	1 tbsp
Apple juice	250 ml	8 fl oz	1 cup
Cider vinegar	120 ml	4 fl oz	½ cup
Paprika	15 ml	1 tbsp	1 tbsp
Chilli powder	5 ml	1 tsp	1 tsp
Salt and freshly ground black pepper			
Skinless chicken breasts, about 175 g/6 oz each	4	4	4
Low-fat spread, melted	15 g	½ oz	1 tbsp
Chopped parsley			
To serve:			
Small jacket-baked potatoes	4	4	4
Broccoli			

1 Mix together all the ingredients, except the chicken breasts, low-fat spread and parsley, in a shallow dish.

2 Add the chicken and turn over in the marinade. Leave to marinate for 2 hours.

3 Remove the chicken and place on a grill (broiler) rack. Brush with half the low-fat spread.

4 Grill (broil) for 10–15 minutes, turning once and brushing with the remaining low-fat spread, until golden and cooked through.

5 Meanwhile, boil the marinade until well reduced. Season and add more sweetener to taste.

6 Transfer the chicken to warmed serving plates and garnish with chopped parsley.

7 Spoon the marinade over and serve each with a small jacket-baked potato and a good portion of broccoli.

PREPARATION TIME:
10 MINUTES,
PLUS MARINATING TIME

COOKING TIME:
15 MINUTES

CALORIES: LESS THAN 350

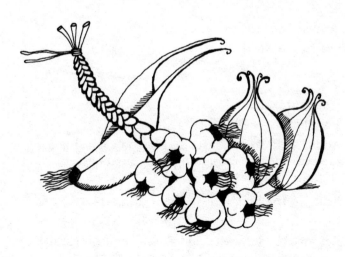

Chicken Paprika

SERVES 4	METRIC	IMPERIAL	AMERICAN
Onions, sliced	2	2	2
Low-fat spread	25 g	1 oz	2 tbsp
Skinless chicken breasts, about 175 g/6 oz each	4	4	4
Paprika	30 ml	2 tbsp	2 tbsp
Can of chopped tomatoes	400 g	14 oz	1 large
Can of pimientos, drained and chopped	228 g	8 oz	1 small
Salt and freshly ground black pepper			
Very low-fat plain yoghurt	45 ml	3 tbsp	3 tbsp
Chopped parsley			

To serve:

Crunchy-topped Tagliatelle (see page 131)

Mixed green salad

1 Fry (sauté) the onions in the low-fat spread in a large saucepan for 2 minutes.

2 Add the chicken breasts and fry on each side to brown. Add the remaining ingredients except the yoghurt and parsley.

3 Bring to the boil, reduce the heat, part-cover and simmer for 10 minutes.

4 Remove the lid, taste and re-season if necessary. Re-cover and simmer for a further 10 minutes.

5 Remove the chicken and transfer to warmed serving plates.

6 Stir the yoghurt into the sauce. Spoon over, garnish with chopped parsley and serve with Crunchy-topped Tagliatelle and a mixed green salad.

PREPARATION TIME:
5 MINUTES

COOKING TIME:
30 MINUTES

CALORIES: LESS THAN 450

Indonesian Supper

SERVES 4	METRIC	IMPERIAL	AMERICAN
Long-grain rice	225 g	8 oz	1 cup
Frozen peas	50 g	2 oz	2 oz
Onions, sliced	2	2	2
Low-fat spread	40 g	1½ oz	3 tbsp
Curry powder	15 ml	1 tbsp	1 tbsp
Ground cinnamon	2.5 ml	½ tsp	½ tsp
Chicken stir-fry meat	175 g	6 oz	6 oz
Cooked ham, diced	50 g	2 oz	½ cup
Salt and freshly ground black pepper			
Egg	1	1	1
Water	30 ml	2 tbsp	2 tbsp
Chopped coriander (cilantro)	30 ml	2 tbsp	2 tbsp

To serve:

Chinese Leaf and Watercress Salad (see page 137)

1 Cook the rice according to the packet directions, adding the peas for the last 5 minutes cooking time. Drain, rinse with cold water and drain again.

2 Meanwhile, fry (sauté) the onions in 25 g/1 oz/ 2 tbsp of the low-fat spread in a large frying pan (skillet) or wok for 2 minutes until softened but not browned.

3 Add the curry powder, cinnamon and chicken and stir-fry for 5 minutes until the chicken is tender and cooked through.

4 Add the ham, rice and peas and toss over a gentle heat for 4 minutes. Season to taste.

5 Meanwhile, beat the egg and water with a little salt and pepper and stir in the coriander.

6 Melt the remaining low-fat spread in an omelette pan and fry the egg mixture until set underneath.

7 Turn over and cook the other side. Roll up and cut into shreds.

8 Pile the rice mixture on to four warmed plates and top with the shredded omelette.

9 Serve with Chinese Leaf and Watercress Salad.

PREPARATION TIME: COOKING TIME:
10 MINUTES 15 MINUTES

CALORIES: LESS THAN 450

Chicken Fajitas

SERVES 4	METRIC	IMPERIAL	AMERICAN
Garlic clove, crushed	1	1	1
Clear honey	15 ml	1 tbsp	1 tbsp
Apple juice	150 ml	¼ pt	⅔ cup
Lager	150 ml	¼ pt	⅔ cup
Red wine vinegar	60 ml	4 tbsp	4 tbsp
Chilli powder	2.5 ml	½ tsp	½ tsp
Chicken stir-fry meat	350 g	12 oz	12 oz
Low-fat spread	25 g	1 oz	2 tbsp
Bunch of spring onions (scallions), diagonally sliced	1	1	1
Red (bell) pepper, cut into thin strips	1	1	1
Green pepper, cut into thin strips	1	1	1
Salt and freshly ground black pepper			
Flour tortillas	8	8	8

To serve:

Lettuce, tomato and cucumber salad

1 Put the garlic, honey, apple juice, lager, vinegar and chilli powder in a pan. Bring to the boil, reduce the heat and simmer for 5 minutes.

2 Put the chicken in a shallow dish. Pour over the marinade and leave to marinate for 1 hour.

3 Heat half the low-fat spread in a large frying pan (skillet). Add the spring onions and peppers and stir-fry for 4 minutes until softened.

4 Remove from the pan and reserve. Add the remaining low-fat spread to the pan.

5 Remove the chicken from the marinade and stir-fry the chicken for 5 minutes until cooked through.

6 Return the spring onions and peppers to the pan with 30 ml/2 tbsp of the marinade and toss until piping hot and glazed. Season to taste.

7 Warm the tortillas according to the packet directions.

8 Divide the chicken mixture between the tortillas. Roll up and serve with salad.

PREPARATION TIME:
10 MINUTES, PLUS
MARINATING TIME

COOKING TIME:
20 MINUTES

CALORIES: LESS THAN 400

Maybe Chicken Chow Mein

SERVES 4	METRIC	IMPERIAL	AMERICAN
Quick-cook Chinese egg noodles	250 g	9 oz	9 oz
Cooked chicken, skin removed, cut into strips	225 g	8 oz	2 cups
Can of stir-fry mixed vegetables, drained	425 g	15 oz	1 large
Garlic clove, crushed	1	1	1
Soy sauce	30 ml	2 tbsp	2 tbsp
Dry sherry	30 ml	2 tbsp	2 tbsp
Ground ginger	5 ml	1 tsp	1 tsp
Artificial sweetener granules			

1 Cook the noodles according to the packet directions. Drain.

2 Put the chicken in a large pan or wok.

3 Rinse the drained can of vegetables in cold water, drain again and add to the chicken with the remaining ingredients, sweetening to taste with sweetener.

4 Heat through, stirring occasionally, until piping hot. Stir in the drained noodles until well coated.

5 Reheat and serve.

PREPARATION TIME: 10 MINUTES COOKING TIME: 5 MINUTES

CALORIES: LESS THAN 350

Chicken with Lime and Garlic

SERVES 4	METRIC	IMPERIAL	AMERICAN
Small skinless chicken breasts	4	4	4
Low-fat spread	50 g	2 oz	¼ cup
Large garlic clove, crushed	1	1	1
Chopped parsley	15 ml	1 tbsp	1 tbsp
Grated rind and juice of 1 lime			
Salt and freshly ground black pepper			
Parsley sprigs			
Basmati rice, boiled	175 g	6 oz	¾ cup
To serve:			
Green Beans with Cherry Tomatoes (see page 138)			

1 Make a slit in the side of each chicken breast to form a pocket.

2 Mash the low-fat spread with the garlic, chopped parsley, lime rind and a little salt and pepper. Spoon into the chicken breasts.

3 Place each on a square of foil and sprinkle with lime juice and a little more salt and pepper. Wrap up.

4 Place on a baking sheet and bake in a preheated oven at 190°C/375°F/gas mark 5 for 30 minutes. Open up the foil after 20 minutes to allow the chicken to brown.

5 Garnish with parsley sprigs and serve with the Basmati rice and Green Beans with Cherry Tomatoes.

PREPARATION TIME:
15 MINUTES

COOKING TIME:
30 MINUTES

CALORIES: LESS THAN 350

Chicken Liver Nests

SERVES 4	METRIC	IMPERIAL	AMERICAN
Potatoes, cut into even-sized pieces	450 g	1 lb	1 lb
Low-fat spread	40 g	1½ oz	3 tbsp
Skimmed milk	15 ml	1 tbsp	1 tbsp
Onions, finely chopped	2	2	2
Wineglass of dry vermouth	1	1	1
Chicken livers, trimmed	450 g	1 lb	4 cups
Chopped sage	5 ml	1 tsp	1 tsp
Salt and freshly ground black pepper			
Frozen leaf spinach	350 g	12 oz	12 oz

1 Boil the potatoes in lightly salted water until tender. Drain and mash with 15 ml/1 tbsp of the low-fat spread and the milk.

2 Spoon into four 'nests' on flameproof serving plates. Flash under a hot grill (broiler) to brown. Keep warm.

3 Meanwhile, melt the remaining low-fat spread in a frying pan (skillet). Add the onions and fry (sauté), stirring, for 4 minutes until golden and soft.

4 Add the vermouth and boil until nearly all the liquid has evaporated.

5 Stir in the chicken livers, sage and a little salt and pepper and cook, stirring, for about 5 minutes until the livers are browned but still tender. Taste and re-season, if necessary.

6 Meanwhile, cook the spinach according to the packet directions. Drain.

7 Spoon the hot livers into the nests and surround with the spinach. Serve straight away.

PREPARATION TIME:
10 MINUTES

COOKING TIME:
20 MINUTES

CALORIES: LESS THAN 350

Gorgeous Glazed Chicken

SERVES 4	METRIC	IMPERIAL	AMERICAN
Skinless chicken breasts, about			
175 g/6 oz each	*4*	*4*	*4*
Low-fat spread	*25 g*	*1 oz*	*2 tbsp*
Dry vermouth	*120 ml*	*4 fl oz*	*½ cup*
Salt and freshly ground black pepper			
Chopped parsley	*15 ml*	*1 tbsp*	*1 tbsp*
To serve:			
Dieter's Rosti (see page 129)			
French (green) beans			

1 Brown the chicken on both sides in the spread.

2 Add the vermouth and a little salt and pepper and cook for 10 minutes.

3 Turn the chicken, add the parsley and cook for 5–10 minutes until cooked through and glazed.

4 Serve with Dieter's Rosti and French beans.

PREPARATION TIME:
5 MINUTES

COOKING TIME:
25 MINUTES

CALORIES: LESS THAN 350

Turkey and Cranberry Burgers

SERVES 4	METRIC	IMPERIAL	AMERICAN
Minced (ground) turkey	450 g	1 lb	4 cups
Small onion, finely chopped	1	1	1
Chopped parsley	15 ml	1 tbsp	1 tbsp
Fresh breadcrumbs	45 ml	3 tbsp	3 tbsp
Grated rind of ½ lemon			
Dried thyme	2.5 ml	½ tsp	½ tsp
Grated nutmeg	1.5 ml	¼ tsp	¼ tsp
Salt and freshly ground black pepper			
Egg, beaten	1	1	1
Cranberry sauce	40 ml	8 tsp	8 tsp
Small slices of bread	4	4	4
Low-fat spread			
Parsley sprigs	4	4	4

To serve:

French-style Peas (see page 127)

1 Mix the turkey with the onion, parsley, breadcrumbs, lemon rind, thyme and nutmeg and season with salt and pepper.

2 Mix with the egg to bind. Shape into eight flat cakes.

3 Put 10 ml/2 tsp cranberry sauce on each of four of the patties. Top with the remaining four and press the edges together well to seal.

4 Grill (broil) on each side for about 5 minutes or until golden brown and cooked through.

5 Meanwhile, cut large rounds from the slices of bread and spread very thinly on both sides with low-fat spread.

6 Fry (sauté) in a frying pan (skillet) until golden brown on both sides. Transfer to four warmed plates.

7 Top each slice with a burger, garnish with a parsley sprig and serve with French-style Peas.

PREPARATION TIME:
15 MINUTES

COOKING TIME:
15 MINUTES

CALORIES: LESS THAN 450

Duck Breasts with Orange

SERVES 4	METRIC	IMPERIAL	AMERICAN
Salt and freshly ground black pepper			
Large duck breasts, skin removed	2	2	2
Low-fat spread	25 g	1 oz	2 tbsp
Brandy	15 ml	1 tbsp	1 tbsp
Chicken stock, made with ½ stock cube	150 ml	¼ pt	⅔ cup
Grated rind and juice of 1 orange			
Cornflour (cornstarch)	15 ml	1 tbsp	1 tbsp
Artificial sweetener granules			
Watercress sprigs			
Orange twists			
To serve:			
New potatoes, scrubbed and boiled	450 g	1 lb	1 lb
Mangetout (snow peas)			

1 Season the duck breasts, then fry (sauté) in the low-fat spread, turning occasionally, for 15 minutes or until cooked to your liking. Transfer to a warmed dish and keep warm.

2 Add the brandy to the pan juices and ignite. When the flames have subsided, add the stock.

3 Blend the orange rind and juice with the cornflour and stir into the pan. Bring to the boil and cook for 1 minute, stirring.

4 Season to taste and sweeten with artificial sweetener.

5 Cut the duck breasts into neat slices. Arrange attractively on four warmed plates.

6 Add any juices to the sauce. Spoon over the duck and garnish each with watercress sprigs and orange twists.

7 Serve hot with new potatoes and mangetout.

PREPARATION TIME:
10 MINUTES

COOKING TIME:
15 MINUTES

CALORIES: LESS THAN 350

Redcurrant Duck

SERVES 4	METRIC	IMPERIAL	AMERICAN
Large duck breasts, skin removed, about 275 g/10 oz each	2	2	2
Low-fat spread	25 g	1 oz	2 tbsp
Port	90 ml	6 tbsp	6 tbsp
Redcurrant jelly (clear conserve)	15 ml	1 tbsp	1 tbsp
Salt and freshly ground black pepper			
Small redcurrant sprigs (optional)	4	4	4
Watercress sprigs			
Potatoes, boiled and garnished with parsley	450 g	1 lb	1 lb

To serve:

Citrus Spinach Salad (see page 140–1)

1 Fry (sauté) the duck breasts in the low-fat spread for about 10–15 minutes until cooked to your liking. Remove from the pan and keep warm.

2 Add the port and redcurrant jelly to the pan and cook, stirring, until the redcurrant jelly dissolves.

3 Boil rapidly until reduced by half. Season to taste.

4 Cut the duck breasts diagonally into neat slices. Arrange on four warmed serving plates.

5 Spoon the sauce over and garnish each with a sprig of redcurrants, if using, and watercress sprigs.

6 Serve with the potatoes and Citrus Spinach Salad.

PREPARATION TIME:
5 MINUTES

COOKING TIME:
20 MINUTES

CALORIES: LESS THAN 350

VEGETARIAN MAIN MEALS

You don't have to be a vegetarian to enjoy a meatless meal. All these recipes are very tasty, wonderfully filling and nutritious. They are, of course, ideal for committed vegetarians but make sure any cheese used is not just reduced-fat, where possible, but also suitable for vegetarians (this is clearly labelled on supermarket packs).

Asparagus and Smoked Tofu Kebabs

SERVES 4	METRIC	IMPERIAL	AMERICAN
Thick asparagus spears, cut into short lengths	225 g	8 oz	8 oz
Smoked tofu, cubed	250 g	9 oz	1 block
Button mushrooms	100 g	4 oz	4 oz
Lime, thinly sliced	1	1	1
Low-fat spread	25 g	1 oz	2 tbsp
Lime juice	10 ml	2 tsp	2 tsp
Salt and freshly ground black pepper			

To serve:

Greek Village Salad (see page 136)

1 Blanch the asparagus in boiling water for 2 minutes. Drain, rinse with cold water and drain again.

2 Thread the tofu, asparagus and mushrooms on soaked wooden skewers, interspersed with lime slices.

3 Melt the low-fat spread with the lime juice and season well. Brush over the kebabs.

4 Grill (broil) for about 8 minutes or until cooked through, turning occasionally and brushing with the melted mixture.

5 Serve with Greek Village Salad.

PREPARATION TIME: 10 MINUTES

COOKING TIME: 15 MINUTES

CALORIES: LESS THAN 350

Instant Veggie Supper

SERVES 4	METRIC	IMPERIAL	AMERICAN
Can of ratatouille	400 g	14 oz	1 large
Can of butter (lima) beans	425 g	15 oz	1 large
Dried mixed herbs	2.5 ml	½ tsp	½ tsp
Salt and freshly ground black pepper			
Fresh breadcrumbs	50 g	2 oz	1 cup
Low-fat Cheddar cheese, grated	50 g	2 oz	½ cup
Eggs	2	2	2
Skimmed milk	30 ml	2 tbsp	2 tbsp
Chopped parsley	15 ml	1 tbsp	1 tbsp
Low-fat spread	5 ml	1 tsp	1 tsp
Parsley sprigs			

1 Heat the ratatouille with the beans, herbs and some pepper in a flameproof casserole (Dutch oven) over a moderate heat.

2 Mix together the breadcrumbs and cheese and sprinkle over. Brown under a hot grill (broiler).

3 Meanwhile, beat together the eggs and milk with a little salt and pepper and the chopped parsley.

4 Melt the low-fat spread in an omelette pan and fry (sauté) the egg mixture until set. Cut into wedges.

5 Serve the ratatouille mixture and omelette garnished with parsley sprigs.

PREPARATION TIME: COOKING TIME:
5 MINUTES 15 MINUTES

CALORIES: LESS THAN 450

Broccoli and Cider Cheese

SERVES 4	METRIC	IMPERIAL	AMERICAN
Broccoli florets	350 g	12 oz	12 oz
Plain (all-purpose) flour	45 ml	3 tbsp	3 tbsp
Skimmed milk powder (non-fat dry milk)	60 ml	4 tbsp	4 tbsp
Cider	150 ml	¼ pt	⅔ cup
A small knob of low-fat spread			
Low-fat Cheddar cheese, grated	50 g	2 oz	½ cup
Salt and freshly ground white pepper			
Eating (dessert) apple, halved, cored and sliced	1	1	1
Lemon juice			
To serve:			
Green Beans with Cherry Tomatoes (see page 138)			
Slices of crusty bread	4	4	4

1 Cook the broccoli in lightly salted boiling water until just tender. Drain, reserving 150 ml/¼ pt/⅔ cup of the cooking water.

2 Place the broccoli in a flameproof serving dish. Blend the flour and milk powder with the cider in the broccoli saucepan until smooth.

3 Stir in the reserved cooking water. Add the low-fat spread.

4 Bring to the boil and cook for 2 minutes, stirring all the time.

5 Stir in three-quarters of the cheese and salt and pepper to taste.

6 Pour over the broccoli. Sprinkle with the remaining cheese and brown under a hot grill (broiler).

7 Dip the apple slices in lemon juice to prevent browning. Arrange attractively around the top of the cheese mixture and serve with Green Beans with Cherry Tomatoes and the bread.

PREPARATION TIME:
10 MINUTES

COOKING TIME:
15 MINUTES

CALORIES: LESS THAN 350

Golden Stuffed Courgettes

SERVES 4	METRIC	IMPERIAL	AMERICAN
Sweetcorn (corn)	175 g	6 oz	6 oz
Very low-fat cottage cheese	100 g	4 oz	½ cup
Small yellow (bell) pepper, finely chopped	1	1	1
Salt and freshly ground black pepper			
Small onion, finely chopped	1	1	1
Chopped parsley	15 ml	1 tbsp	1 tbsp
Large courgettes (zucchini)	4	4	4
Low-fat spread	5 ml	1 tsp	1 tsp
Grated Parmesan cheese (fresh if possible)	45 ml	3 tbsp	3 tbsp
Tomato slices			
To serve:			
Nutty Wild Rice Mix (see page 133)			

1 Mix together the corn, cottage cheese, yellow pepper, a little salt and pepper, the onion and parsley.

2 Halve the courgettes lengthways and scoop out the seeds with a teaspoon.

3 Spoon the cottage cheese mixture into the courgettes, piling them up a little.

4 Grease a shallow baking dish with the low-fat spread and place the stuffed courgettes in it in a single layer.

5 Sprinkle the Parmesan over. Bake in a preheated oven at 200°C/400°F/gas mark 6 for about 20 minutes until the courgettes are tender and the topping is lightly golden.

6 Transfer to warmed plates, garnish with tomato slices and serve with Nutty Wild Rice Mix.

PREPARATION TIME:
15 MINUTES

COOKING TIME:
20 MINUTES

CALORIES: LESS THAN 350

Simple Stuffed Peppers

SERVES 4	METRIC	IMPERIAL	AMERICAN
Red (bell) peppers	4	4	4
Packet of diced frozen mixed vegetables	227 g	8 oz	1 small
Spring onion (scallion), finely chopped	1	1	1
Button mushrooms, chopped	50 g	2 oz	2 oz
Fresh wholemeal or rye breadcrumbs	25 g	1 oz	½ cup
Low-fat Cheddar cheese, grated	50 g	2 oz	½ cup
Small egg	1	1	1
Light soy sauce	15 ml	1 tbsp	1 tbsp
Salt and freshly ground black pepper			
To serve:			
Brown rice, boiled	175 g	6 oz	¾ cup
Mixed green salad			

1 Cut the tops off the peppers and discard the seeds and membranes inside. Trim the bases carefully so they stand up but without making any holes.

2 Cook the peppers and the tops in boiling water for 8 minutes. Drain and stand in a roasting tin (pan).

3 Meanwhile, cook the vegetables according to the packet directions, but using only enough water to cover the vegetables. Add the onion and mushrooms for the last minute of cooking.

4 Drain and mix with the breadcrumbs and cheese.

5 Beat the egg with the soy sauce and stir into the vegetable mixture. Season lightly.

6 Pack into the peppers, top with the 'lids' and bake in a preheated oven at 190°C/375°F/gas mark 5 for about 20 minutes until tender.

7 Serve with the rice and a mixed green salad.

PREPARATION TIME:
10 MINUTES

COOKING TIME:
30 MINUTES

CALORIES: LESS THAN 350

Oven-baked Pilau

SERVES 4	METRIC	IMPERIAL	AMERICAN
Bunch of spring onions (scallions), chopped	1	1	1
Garlic clove, crushed	1	1	1
Low-fat spread	25 g	1 oz	2 tbsp
Long-grain rice	225 g	8 oz	1 cup
Vegetable stock, made with 2 stock cubes	600 ml	1 pt	2½ cups
Bouquet garni sachet	1	1	1
Button mushrooms	175 g	6 oz	6 oz
Frozen peas with sweetcorn (corn)	225 g	8 oz	8 oz
Salt and freshly ground black pepper			
Pine nuts	30 ml	2 tbsp	2 tbsp
Tomatoes, cut into wedges	4	4	4
Parsley sprigs			

1 Fry (sauté) the spring onions and garlic in the low-fat spread in a flameproof casserole (Dutch oven) for 2 minutes, stirring.

2 Stir in the rice and cook for 1 minute. Add the stock, bouquet garni, mushrooms and the peas and sweetcorn. Season well. Bring to the boil, cover and cook in a preheated oven at 200°C/400°F/gas mark 6 for 20 minutes until the rice is tender and has absorbed the liquid.

3 Taste and re-season, if necessary. Discard the bouquet garni. Fluff up with a fork and sprinkle with the pine nuts.

4 Arrange the tomato wedges around and garnish with a few parsley sprigs. Serve straight away.

PREPARATION TIME:
10 MINUTES

COOKING TIME:
30 MINUTES

CALORIES: LESS THAN 350

Chick Pea Curry

SERVES 4	METRIC	IMPERIAL	AMERICAN
Garlic clove, crushed	1	1	1
Ground ginger	5 ml	1 tsp	1 tsp
Ground coriander (cilantro)	5 ml	1 tsp	1 tsp
Chilli powder	1.5 ml	¼ tsp	¼ tsp
Turmeric	1.5 ml	¼ tsp	¼ tsp
Water	15 ml	1 tbsp	1 tbsp
Low-fat spread	25 g	1 oz	2 tbsp
Onion, finely chopped	1	1	1
Curry paste	10 ml	2 tsp	2 tsp
Can of chopped tomatoes	400 g	14 oz	1 large
Cans of chick peas (garbanzos), drained	2×430 g	2×15½ oz	2 large
Salt and freshly ground black pepper			
A few torn coriander leaves, lettuce leaves and lemon wedges			
Desiccated (shredded) coconut	60 ml	4 tbsp	4 tbsp
To serve:			
Packet of pilau rice, boiled	1	1	1

1 Mix together the garlic and spices with the water.

2 Melt the low-fat spread in a saucepan and add the onion. Fry (sauté) for 3 minutes.

3 Add the spice mixture and the curry paste and fry for 1 minute.

4 Add the tomatoes and chick peas and simmer for 15 minutes until bathed in sauce. Season to taste.

5 Spoon on to warmed plates, garnish with coriander leaves, lettuce leaves and lemon wedges and sprinkle with the coconut.

6 Serve with pilau rice.

PREPARATION TIME:	COOKING TIME:
10 MINUTES	20 MINUTES

CALORIES: LESS THAN 550

Baked Bean Loaf

SERVES 4	METRIC	IMPERIAL	AMERICAN
Low-fat spread	10 ml	2 tsp	2 tsp
Can of no-added-sugar baked beans	400 g	14 oz	1 large
Small onion, finely chopped	1	1	1
Wholemeal breadcrumbs	50 g	2 oz	1 cup
Reduced sugar and salt tomato ketchup (catsup)	30 ml	2 tbsp	2 tbsp
Egg, beaten	1	1	1
Yeast extract	5 ml	1 tsp	1 tsp
Dried mixed herbs	5 ml	1 tsp	1 tsp
Salt and freshly ground black pepper			
Lettuce leaves and tomato wedges			
To serve:			
Small jacket-baked potatoes	4	4	4
Beetroot and Orange Salad (see page 139)			

1 Mix together all the ingredients. Turn into a wetted and lined 450 g/1 lb loaf tin (pan). Level the top.

2 Bake in a preheated oven at 180°C/350°F/gas mark 4 for 30–40 minutes until firm to the touch. Cool in the tin for a few minutes, then turn out.

3 Serve warm or cold, sliced, garnished with lettuce leaves and tomato wedges, with a small jacket-baked potato and Beetroot and Orange Salad.

PREPARATION TIME:
10 MINUTES

COOKING TIME:
30–40 MINUTES

CALORIES: LESS THAN 450

Greek Chick Pea Casserole

SERVES 4	METRIC	IMPERIAL	AMERICAN
Low-fat spread	25 g	1 oz	2 tbsp
Spinach, washed and shredded	450 g	1 lb	1 lb
Garlic clove, crushed	1	1	1
Can of chick peas (garbanzos), drained	450 g	15 oz	1 large
Feta cheese, cubed	100 g	4 oz	1 cup
Salt and freshly ground black pepper			
A pinch of ground cinnamon			
Tomatoes, skinned, seeded and chopped	4	4	4
Very low-fat crème fraîche	120 ml	4 fl oz	1 cup
Small pitta breads	8	8	8
To serve:			
Mixed green salad			

1 Heat the low-fat spread and fry (sauté) the spinach and garlic, stirring, for 4 minutes. Add the chick peas, cheese, salt, pepper and cinnamon. Toss over a gentle heat for 2 minutes. Add the tomatoes and crème fraîche and heat through, stirring.

2 Warm the pitta breads briefly to puff them up. Make a slit along the top of each one to form a pocket.

3 Fill with the spinach and serve with a green salad.

PREPARATION TIME: 15 MINUTES COOKING TIME: 10 MINUTES

CALORIES: LESS THAN 450

Mediterranean Haricots

SERVES 4	METRIC	IMPERIAL	AMERICAN
Large onions, sliced	2	2	2
Garlic cloves, crushed	2	2	2
Low-fat spread	25 g	1 oz	2 tbsp
Cans of haricot (navy) beans, drained	2×425 g	2×15 oz	2 large
Can of chopped tomatoes	400 g	14 oz	1 large
Sun-dried tomatoes, chopped	2	2	2
Chopped basil	15 ml	1 tbsp	1 tbsp
Salt and freshly ground black pepper			
A few torn basil leaves			
Black olives, stoned (pitted) and halved	8	8	8
To serve:			
Plain pasta, cooked	225 g	8 oz	8 oz
Mixed salad			

1 Fry (sauté) the onions and garlic in the low-fat spread for 3 minutes.

2 Add all the remaining ingredients except the torn basil leaves and olives.

3 Bring to the boil, reduce the heat and simmer for about 10 minutes until it forms a rich sauce.

4 Serve, garnished with torn basil leaves and olives, on a bed of pasta with a mixed salad.

PREPARATION TIME: 15 MINUTES

COOKING TIME: 15 MINUTES

CALORIES: LESS THAN 450

SIDE DISHES AND SALADS

If you don't fancy a lavishly cooked meal, you may prefer a plain grilled piece of meat or fish with an exciting side dish. So you can calculate your whole meal, here are some calorie counts for plain grilled meats and fish (trim off all fat):

150 calories or less: *white fish fillet or small whole plaice (about 175g/6 oz); 2 chicken drumsticks, skin removed*

200 calories or less: *skinless, boneless turkey steak or chicken breast (about 175 g/6 oz)*

250 calories or less: *2 large pork sausages; salmon or other oily fish steak; lamb chop, cutlets or leg steak, pork chop or steak (about 175 g/6 oz)*

300 calories or less: *gammon or bacon steak (about 175 g/6 oz)*

350 calories or less: *fillet, rump or sirloin steak (about 175 g/6 oz); average-sized mackerel or other oily fish*

Saucy Runner Beans

SERVES 4	METRIC	IMPERIAL	AMERICAN
Runner beans, stringed and diagonally sliced	350 g	12 oz	12 oz
Low-fat spread	15 g	½ oz	1 tbsp
Plain (all-purpose) flour	15 g	½ oz	2 tbsp
Vegetable stock, made with 1 stock cube	250 ml	8 fl oz	1 cup
Bay leaf	1	1	1
Very low-fat crème fraîche	30 ml	2 tbsp	2 tbsp
Chopped parsley	30 ml	2 tbsp	2 tbsp
Salt and freshly ground black pepper			

1 Cook the beans in boiling, lightly salted water until just tender. Drain.

2 Melt the low-fat spread in the saucepan. Add the flour and cook for 1 minute.

3 Remove from the heat and blend in the stock.

4 Add the bay leaf, bring to the boil and cook for 2 minutes, stirring all the time, until thick and smooth.

5 Stir in the crème fraîche, parsley and seasoning to taste.

6 Discard the bay leaf. Add the beans, toss in the sauce and serve hot.

PREPARATION TIME: 10 MINUTES

COOKING TIME: 10 MINUTES

CALORIES: LESS THAN 50

French-style Peas

SERVES 4	METRIC	IMPERIAL	AMERICAN
Round lettuce, shredded	½	½	½
Bunch of spring onions (scallions), cut into short lengths	1	1	1
Chopped mint	5 ml	1 tsp	1 tsp
Chopped parsley	5 ml	1 tsp	1 tsp
Frozen peas	450 g	1 lb	1 lb
Vegetable stock, made with ½ stock cube	150 ml	¼ pt	⅔ cup
Low-fat spread	40 g	1½ oz	3 tbsp
Salt and freshly ground black pepper			
A pinch of artificial sweetener granules			
Chopped parsley			

1 Put the lettuce in a pan with the spring onions, chopped herbs, peas, stock and low-fat spread.

2 Sprinkle with a little salt and pepper and a pinch of sweetener.

3 Bring to the boil, cover tightly and simmer for 30 minutes. Taste and re-season if necessary.

4 Serve garnished with chopped parsley.

PREPARATION TIME:
10 MINUTES

COOKING TIME:
35 MINUTES

CALORIES: LESS THAN 150

Fruity Red Cabbage

SERVES 4	METRIC	IMPERIAL	AMERICAN
Red cabbage, shredded	450 g	1 lb	1 lb
Onion, sliced	1	1	1
Eating (dessert) apple, sliced	1	1	1
Sultanas (golden raisins)	50 g	2 oz	⅓ cup
Salt and freshly ground black pepper			
Vinegar	30 ml	2 tbsp	2 tbsp
Water	30 ml	2 tbsp	2 tbsp
Artificial sweetener granules			
Low-fat spread	25 g	1 oz	2 tbsp

1 Layer the cabbage, onion, apple and sultanas in a casserole dish (Dutch oven), seasoning each layer with a little salt and pepper.

2 Mix together the vinegar, water and artificial sweetener to taste and pour over. Dot with the low-fat spread.

3 Cover with a piece of greaseproof (waxed) paper, then the lid.

4 Bake in a preheated oven at 180°C/350°F/gas mark 4 for about 1–1½ hours until tender. (The cabbage can be cooked for longer in a slower oven or quicker in a higher one, depending on what else you are cooking at the same time.)

5 Stir well before serving.

PREPARATION TIME: 10 MINUTES

COOKING TIME: 1–1½ HOURS

CALORIES: LESS THAN 150

Dieter's Rosti

SERVES 4	METRIC	IMPERIAL	AMERICAN
Potatoes, scrubbed	450 g	1 lb	1 lb
Low-fat spread	40 g	1½ oz	3 tbsp
Onion, finely chopped	1	1	1
Salt and freshly ground black pepper			
Parsley sprigs			

1 Boil the potatoes in their skins until just tender.
   Drain.

2 When cool enough to handle, peel and coarsely grate.

3 Melt half the low-fat spread in a frying pan (skillet).
   Add the onion and fry (sauté) for 3 minutes until
   softened but not browned.

4 Add the potato and some salt and pepper and press
   down well.

5 Cook over a fairly low heat for about 20 minutes
   until golden brown. Turn the potato cake out on to a
   plate.

6 Melt the remaining low-fat spread in the pan. Slide
   in the rosti, browned side up, and continue cooking
   for a further 10 minutes or until golden underneath.

7 Serve in wedges, garnished with parsley sprigs.

PREPARATION TIME:
10 MINUTES

COOKING TIME:
45 MINUTES

CALORIES: LESS THAN 150

Oriental Rice and Peas

SERVES 4	METRIC	IMPERIAL	AMERICAN
Thai fragrant rice	175 g	6 oz	¾ cup
Frozen peas	75 g	3 oz	3 oz
Ground ginger	1.5 ml	¼ tsp	¼ tsp
Light soy sauce	30 ml	2 tbsp	2 tbsp
Spring onions (scallions), chopped	2	2	2

1 Cook the rice according to the packet directions, adding the peas for the last 5 minutes cooking time. Drain and return to the pan.

2 Add the ginger and soy sauce, toss and serve garnished with the spring onions.

PREPARATION TIME:
5 MINUTES

COOKING TIME:
15 MINUTES

CALORIES: LESS THAN 150

Crunchy-topped Tagliatelle

SERVES 4	METRIC	IMPERIAL	AMERICAN
Tagliatelle	225 g	8 oz	8 oz
Fresh breadcrumbs	25 g	1 oz	½ cup
Low-fat spread	25 g	1 oz	2 tbsp
Garlic powder	2.5 ml	½ tsp	½ tsp
Salt and freshly ground black pepper			

1 Cook the pasta according to the packet directions. Drain and return to the saucepan.

2 Meanwhile, melt the low-fat spread in a frying pan (skillet). Add the breadcrumbs, garlic powder and a little salt and pepper.

3 Fry (sauté), stirring, until golden brown and crisp.

4 Add to the tagliatelle, toss and serve straight away.

PREPARATION TIME:
5 MINUTES

COOKING TIME:
10 MINUTES

CALORIES: LESS THAN 250

Tomatoes with Courgettes

SERVES 4	METRIC	IMPERIAL	AMERICAN
Can of chopped tomatoes	400 g	14 oz	1 large
Garlic clove, crushed	1	1	1
Artificial sweetener granules			
Salt and freshly ground black pepper			
Dried oregano	2.5 ml	½ tsp	½ tsp
Courgettes (zucchini), sliced	6	6	6

1 Put the tomatoes in a pan with the garlic, a very few grains of sweetener, some salt and pepper and the oregano.

2 Bring to the boil and simmer for 3 minutes.

3 Add the courgettes and simmer, uncovered, for about 15–20 minutes until the courgettes are tender and bathed in a rich sauce.

4 Taste and re-season, if necessary.

PREPARATION TIME:
5 MINUTES

COOKING TIME:
25 MINUTES

CALORIES: LESS THAN 50

Nutty Wild Rice Mix

SERVES 4	METRIC	IMPERIAL	AMERICAN
Wild rice mix	*175 g*	*6 oz*	*¾ cup*
Frozen peas	*50 g*	*2 oz*	*2 oz*
Low-fat spread	*40 g*	*1½ oz*	*3 tbsp*
Toasted mixed nuts	*50 g*	*2 oz*	*½ cup*
Chopped thyme	*15 ml*	*1 tbsp*	*1 tbsp*
Salt and freshly ground black pepper			

1 Cook the rice according to the packet directions, adding the peas for the last 5 minutes cooking time. Drain and return to the pan.

2 Add the low-fat spread, nuts and thyme and season to taste with salt and pepper.

3 Toss well and serve.

PREPARATION TIME:
5 MINUTES

COOKING TIME:
20 MINUTES

CALORIES: LESS THAN 250

Baked Tomatoes with Spring Onions

SERVES 4	METRIC	IMPERIAL	AMERICAN
Tomatoes, halved	8	8	8
Low-fat spread	25 g	1 oz	2 tbsp
Bunch of spring onions (scallions), chopped	1	1	1
Salt and freshly ground black pepper			
Chopped parsley	15 ml	1 tbsp	1 tbsp

1 Place the tomatoes in a shallow ovenproof dish.

2 Melt the low-fat spread in a frying pan (skillet), add the spring onions and fry (sauté) for 3 minutes, stirring.

3 Spoon over the tomatoes, sprinkle with salt and pepper and the parsley.

4 Cover with foil and bake in a preheated oven at 180°C/350°F/gas mark 4 for about 20 minutes until soft.

5 Serve straight from the dish.

PREPARATION TIME: 5 MINUTES

COOKING TIME: 25 MINUTES

CALORIES: LESS THAN 50

Garlic Bread

SERVES 4	METRIC	IMPERIAL	AMERICAN
Small French stick	*1*	*1*	*1*
Low-fat spread	*75 g*	*3 oz*	*⅓ cup*
Garlic clove, crushed	*1*	*1*	*1*
Chopped parsley	*15 ml*	*1 tbsp*	*1 tbsp*

1 Cut the bread into eight slices, not quite through the base.

2 Mash the low-fat spread with the garlic and parsley. Spread between the cuts. Spread any remainder over the top.

3 Wrap in foil and bake in a preheated oven at 200°C/400°F/gas mark 6 for about 15 minutes or until the crust is crisp and the centre feels soft when squeezed.

4 Serve hot.

PREPARATION TIME: 10 MINUTES

COOKING TIME: 15 MINUTES

CALORIES: LESS THAN 250

Walnut Bread

SERVES 4

Prepare as for Garlic Bread, but substitute 20 ml/4 tsp chopped walnuts for the garlic.

Greek Village Salad

SERVES 4	METRIC	IMPERIAL	AMERICAN
Iceberg lettuce, shredded	½	½	½
Small white cabbage, shredded	¼	¼	¼
Beefsteak or plum tomatoes, halved and sliced	2	2	2
Piece of cucumber, diced	5 cm	2 in	2 in
Small red onion, sliced and separated into rings	1	1	1
Feta cheese, cubed	100 g	4 oz	1 cup
Black olives	8	8	8
Olive oil	25 ml	1½ tbsp	1½ tbsp
Red wine vinegar	15 ml	1 tbsp	1 tbsp
Dried oregano	5 ml	1 tsp	1 tsp
Salt and freshly ground black pepper			

1 Mix the lettuce and cabbage in a large shallow serving bowl.

2 Scatter the tomatoes, cucumber, onion, cheese and olives over.

3 Drizzle with the oil and vinegar and sprinkle with the oregano and salt and pepper.

PREPARATION TIME:
20 MINUTES

CALORIES: LESS THAN 150

Chinese Leaf and Watercress Salad

SERVES 4	METRIC	IMPERIAL	AMERICAN
Small head of Chinese leaves (stem lettuce), cut into chunks	½	½	½
Bunch of watercress	1	1	1
Sesame oil	10 ml	2 tsp	2 tsp
Cider vinegar	15 ml	1 tbsp	1 tbsp
A dash of soy sauce			
Freshly ground black pepper			
Sesame seeds, toasted	15 ml	1 tbsp	1 tbsp

1 Put the Chinese leaves in a bowl.

2 Trim off any feathery stalks from the watercress, pull into small sprigs and add to the Chinese leaves.

3 Whisk together the sesame oil, cider vinegar, soy sauce and some pepper.

4 Drizzle over, toss and sprinkle with sesame seeds before serving.

PREPARATION TIME:
10 MINUTES

CALORIES: LESS THAN 50

Green Beans with Cherry Tomatoes

SERVES 4	METRIC	IMPERIAL	AMERICAN
Thin French (green) beans, topped and tailed but left whole	225 g	8 oz	8 oz
Cherry tomatoes, halved	225 g	8 oz	8 oz
Small red onion, finely chopped	1	1	1
Red wine vinegar	30 ml	2 tbsp	2 tbsp
Olive oil	15 ml	1 tbsp	1 tbsp
A pinch of artificial sweetener granules			
Dijon mustard	2.5 ml	½ tsp	½ tsp
Salt and freshly ground black pepper			

1 Cook the beans in boiling, lightly salted water until tender. Drain, rinse with cold water and drain again.

2 Lay in a shallow serving dish and scatter the tomatoes over. Sprinkle with the chopped onion.

3 Whisk together the remaining ingredients and drizzle over.

4 Leave to stand for 30 minutes before serving.

PREPARATION TIME:
10 MINUTES,
PLUS STANDING TIME

COOKING TIME:
5 MINUTES

CALORIES: LESS THAN 50

Beetroot and Orange Salad

SERVES 4	METRIC	IMPERIAL	AMERICAN
Little Gem lettuce, separated into leaves	1	1	1
Oranges	2	2	2
Large cooked beetroot (red beets), diced	2	2	2
Orange juice	15 ml	1 tbsp	1 tbsp
Balsamic vinegar	5 ml	1 tsp	1 tsp
Salt and freshly ground black pepper			
Snipped chives			

1 Arrange the lettuce leaves on four small plates.

2 Holding the fruit over a bowl, remove all pith and rind from the oranges and cut into segments.

3 Squeeze the membranes over the bowl to extract all the juice.

4 Pile the beetroot in the centre of the lettuce with the orange segments around.

5 Add the measured orange juice to the bowl with the balsamic vinegar. Season to taste.

6 Spoon over and garnish the beetroot with a few snipped chives.

PREPARATION TIME:
15 MINUTES

CALORIES: LESS THAN 50

Citrus Spinach Salad

SERVES 4	METRIC	IMPERIAL	AMERICAN
Young spinach leaves	225 g	8 oz	8 oz
Pink grapefruit	1	1	1
Orange	1	1	1
Onion, thinly sliced and separated into rings	1	1	1
For the dressing:			
White wine vinegar	30 ml	2 tbsp	2 tbsp
Water	15 ml	1 tbsp	1 tbsp
Dijon mustard	2.5 ml	½ tsp	½ tsp
Chopped parsley	5 ml	1 tsp	1 tsp
Chopped tarragon	5 ml	1 tsp	1 tsp
Artificial sweetener granules			
Salt and freshly ground black pepper			

1 Thoroughly wash the spinach, pat dry and remove any damaged stalks. Tear the leaves into smaller pieces, if liked. Arrange on four small serving plates.

2 Holding the fruit over a bowl, remove all pith and rind from the grapefruit and orange and separate the fruit into segments between the membranes.

3 Squeeze the membranes over the bowl to extract all the juice.

4 Lay the fruit on the spinach and scatter the onion rings over.

5 To make the dressing, whisk together the wine vinegar, water and mustard. Mix in the citrus juices, then stir in the herbs. Sweeten and season to taste.

6 Spoon the dressing over the salad and chill, if time, before serving.

PREPARATION TIME:
15 MINUTES,
PLUS CHILLING TIME

CALORIES: LESS THAN 50

Crunchy Carrot Salad

SERVES 4

Large carrots, grated	4	4	4
Celery sticks, finely chopped	2	2	2
Raisins	30 ml	1 tbsp	1 tbsp
Snipped chives	30 ml	2 tbsp	2 tbsp
Walnut oil	10 ml	2 tsp	2 tsp
Orange juice	20 ml	4 tsp	4 tsp
Salt and freshly ground black pepper			
Large lettuce leaves	4	4	4
Walnut halves	4	4	4

1 Mix together the carrots, celery, raisins and chives.

2 Whisk the oil with the juice, salt and pepper.

3 Pour over the salad and toss well.

4 Pile on to lettuce leaves and garnish each with a walnut half.

PREPARATION TIME:
10 MINUTES

CALORIES: LESS THAN 100

Chinese Prawn Salad

SERVES 6	METRIC	IMPERIAL	AMERICAN
Bean sprouts	175 g	6 oz	6 oz
Small red (bell) pepper, chopped	1	1	1
Peeled prawns (shrimp)	100 g	4 oz	4 oz
Soy sauce	10 ml	2 tsp	2 tsp
White wine vinegar	10 ml	2 tsp	2 tsp
A pinch of artificial sweetener granules			
Sesame oil	30 ml	2 tbsp	2 tbsp
Salt and freshly ground black pepper			
Large lettuce leaves	6	6	6
Spring onion (scallion), chopped	1	1	1

1 Put the bean sprouts in a bowl with the chopped pepper and prawns.

2 Mix together all the remaining ingredients except the lettuce and spring onion and pour over. Toss well.

3 Spoon on to the lettuce leaves on six individual serving plates and sprinkle each portion with a little of the spring onion.

PREPARATION TIME:
10 MINUTES

CALORIES: LESS THAN 100

DESSERTS

*For many of us, a meal is not complete
without a pud. Some of these will be old
favourites, carefully re-created so you can
enjoy them even on a diet! If you aren't
having one of these delicious concoctions,
treat yourself to some seasonal or exotic fresh
fruit, prepared appropriately and arranged
attractively on a plate. Eat slowly and enjoy.*

Bananas with Hot Lemon Sauce

SERVES 4	METRIC	IMPERIAL	AMERICAN
Low-fat spread	15 g	½ oz	1 tbsp
Artificial sweetener granules	10 ml	2 tsp	2 tsp
Cornflour (cornstarch)	15 ml	1 tbsp	1 tbsp
Grated rind and juice of ½ lemon			
Small bananas	4	4	4
Very low-fat plain yoghurt	300 ml	½ pt	1¼ cups
Ground cinnamon			

1 Put the low-fat spread, sweetener and cornflour in a saucepan.

2 Make the lemon juice up to 150 ml/¼ pt/⅔ cup with water. Stir into the pan.

3 Bring to the boil and cook, stirring, for 2 minutes.

4 Peel and slice the bananas.

5 Spoon the yoghurt into four small dishes and top with the bananas.

6 Spoon the hot sauce over and dust with cinnamon. Serve straight away.

PREPARATION TIME:
10 MINUTES

COOKING TIME:
5 MINUTES

CALORIES: LESS THAN 100

Baked Stuffed Peaches

SERVES 4	METRIC	IMPERIAL	AMERICAN
Ripe peaches, halved and stoned (pitted)	4	4	4
Can of raspberries in natural juice, drained and juice reserved	300 g	11 oz	1 medium
Artificial sweetener granules	5 ml	1 tsp	1 tsp
Desiccated (shredded) coconut	15 ml	1 tbsp	1 tbsp
Breadcrumbs	15 ml	1 tbsp	1 tbsp
Low-fat spread	10 ml	2 tsp	2 tsp

1 Place the peaches, cut sides up, in a shallow ovenproof dish. Put the drained raspberries in the cavities. Pour the juice around.

2 Mix the sweetener with the coconut and breadcrumbs. Sprinkle on top of the peaches and dot with the low-fat spread.

3 Bake in a preheated oven at 190°C/375°F/gas mark 5 for about 25 minutes until hot through and the tops are turning brown.

PREPARATION TIME: 10 MINUTES COOKING TIME: 25 MINUTES

CALORIES: LESS THAN 100

Hot Strawberry Roll

SERVES 6	METRIC	IMPERIAL	AMERICAN
Strawberries	175 g	6 oz	6 oz
Lemon juice	2.5 ml	½ tsp	½ tsp
Artificial sweetener granules			
Eggs	2	2	2
Plain (all-purpose) flour	50 g	2 oz	½ cup
Hot water	15 ml	1 tbsp	1 tbsp
Reduced-sugar strawberry jam (conserve)	30 ml	2 tbsp	2 tbsp

1 Purée the strawberries in a blender or food processor. Turn into a small saucepan and add the lemon juice. Sweeten to taste. Heat through.

2 Dampen an 18 × 28 cm/7 × 11 in Swiss roll tin (jelly roll pan) and line with non-stick baking parchment.

3 Break the eggs in a bowl, add 10 ml/2 tsp artificial sweetener granules, place over a pan of gently simmering water and whisk until thick and pale. Sift the flour over the surface and fold in with a metal spoon, adding the hot water.

4 Turn into the prepared tin and gently spread out evenly. Bake in a preheated oven at 200°C/400°F/gas mark 6 for 8–10 minutes until golden and the centre springs back when lightly pressed with a finger.

5 Turn out on to a clean sheet of baking parchment and spread quickly with the jam. Make a mark with the back of a knife about 1 cm/½ in from one short end. Fold this over firmly, then roll up with the help of the baking parchment.

6 Cut into six slices. Transfer to warmed plates, spoon the warm strawberry sauce to one side and serve.

PREPARATION TIME:
25 MINUTES

COOKING TIME:
10 MINUTES

CALORIES: LESS THAN 100

Hot Mocha Custard

SERVES 4	METRIC	IMPERIAL	AMERICAN
Cornflour (cornstarch)	*30 ml*	*2 tbsp*	*2 tbsp*
Cocoa (unsweetened chocolate) *powder*	*30 ml*	*2 tbsp*	*2 tbsp*
Skimmed milk	*300 ml*	*½ pt*	*1¼ cups*
Strong black coffee	*300 ml*	*½ pt*	*1¼ cups*
Artificial sweetener granules			

1 Put the cornflour and cocoa in a pan with a little of the milk and blend until smooth. Blend in the remaining milk and coffee.

2 Bring to the boil and cook for 3 minutes, stirring, until thick and smooth. Sweeten to taste.

3 Spoon into serving dishes and serve straight away.

PREPARATION TIME:
5 MINUTES

COOKING TIME:
5 MINUTES

CALORIES: LESS THAN 100

Profiteroles with Hot Chocolate Sauce

SERVES 4	METRIC	IMPERIAL	AMERICAN
Plain (all-purpose) flour	65 g	2½ oz	generous ½ cup
A pinch of salt			
Water	150 ml	¼ pt	⅔ cup
Low-fat spread	50 g	2 oz	¼ cup
Eggs, beaten	2	2	2
Low-fat whipping cream, whipped	150 ml	¼ pt	⅔ cup
Cocoa (unsweetened chocolate) powder	15 ml	1 tbsp	1 tbsp
Artificial sweetener granules	10–15 ml	2–3 tsp	2–3 tsp
Skimmed milk	15 ml	1 tbsp	1 tbsp

1 Sift the flour and salt twice on to a sheet of kitchen paper (paper towel).

2 Put the water and half the low-fat spread in a saucepan and heat until the spread melts. Add all the flour in one go and beat with a wooden spoon until the mixture leaves the sides of the pan clean. Remove from the heat.

3 Cool slightly, then beat in the eggs a little at a time until the mixture is smooth and glossy but still holds its shape (you may not need quite all the egg).

4 Line a baking sheet with non-stick baking parchment. Put spoonfuls of the mixture on the paper, a little apart to allow for rising. Bake in a preheated oven at 200°C/400°F/gas mark 6 for about 15–20 minutes until risen, crisp and golden.

5 Transfer to a wire rack to cool. Make a slit in the side of each one and fill with a little of the whipped cream.

6 Put the remaining low-fat spread in a saucepan with the cocoa, sweetener to taste and the milk. Heat gently, stirring, until melted and smooth.

7 Put the profiteroles in four serving dishes. Spoon the hot chocolate sauce over and serve.

PREPARATION TIME: COOKING TIME:
30 MINUTES   30–35 MINUTES

CALORIES: LESS THAN 200

Baked Satsumas in Brandy

SERVES 4	METRIC	IMPERIAL	AMERICAN
Orange juice	45 ml	3 tbsp	3 tbsp
Artificial sweetener granules	5 ml	1 tsp	1 tsp
Low-fat spread	25 g	1 oz	2 tbsp
Brandy	30 ml	2 tbsp	2 tbsp
Small satsumas or clementines, peeled and all pith removed	8	8	8

1 Put the orange juice, sweetener, low-fat spread and brandy in a flameproof casserole dish (Dutch oven). Bring to the boil and simmer for 2 minutes.

2 Add the fruit and turn in the liquid.

3 Cover and bake in a preheated oven at 180°C/350°F/ gas mark 4 for about 30 minutes until just cooked, spooning the juices over twice during cooking.

PREPARATION TIME: COOKING TIME:
10 MINUTES · 35 MINUTES

CALORIES: LESS THAN 100

Orange Baked Custard

SERVES 4	METRIC	IMPERIAL	AMERICAN
Eggs	2	2	2
Artificial sweetener granules	5 ml	1 tsp	1 tsp
Finely grated rind of 1 orange			
Skimmed milk, warmed	450 ml	¾ pt	2 cups
Ground cinnamon			

1 Beat the eggs with the artificial sweetener and the orange rind. Whisk in the warm milk. Taste and add a little more sweetener, if liked.

2 Strain into an ovenproof dish and dust with cinnamon. Transfer to a roasting tin (pan) containing 2.5 cm/1 in cold water.

3 Bake in a preheated oven at 150°C/300°F/gas mark 2 for about 1 hour or until set.

4 Serve warm.

PREPARATION TIME: 10 MINUTES

COOKING TIME: 1 HOUR

CALORIES: LESS THAN 100

Venetian Coffee Cheese

SERVES 6	METRIC	IMPERIAL	AMERICAN
Instant coffee granules	15 ml	1 tbsp	1 tbsp
Water	15 ml	1 tbsp	1 tbsp
Very low-fat soft cheese	225 g	8 oz	1 cup
Artificial sweetener granules			
Walnut halves	6	6	6
To serve:			
Ice-cream wafers	12	12	12

1 Mix the coffee with the water until dissolved.

2 Gradually beat into the cheese with sweetener to taste.

3 Turn into six very small serving pots and top each with a walnut half.

4 Chill until ready to serve with the wafers.

PREPARATION TIME:
10 MINUTES,
PLUS CHILLING TIME

CALORIES: LESS THAN 100

Apple and Blackcurrant Kissel

SERVES 4	METRIC	IMPERIAL	AMERICAN
Large cooking (tart) apples, sliced	2	2	2
Blackcurrants	100 g	4 oz	4 oz
Artificial sweetener granules	10 ml	2 tsp	2 tsp
Port	75 ml	5 tbsp	5 tbsp
Piece of cinnamon stick	1	1	1
Arrowroot	10 ml	2 tsp	2 tsp
Water	15 ml	1 tbsp	1 tbsp

1 Put the apples and blackcurrants in a saucepan with the sweetener and the port. Add the cinnamon. Cover and cook gently until the fruit is tender, stirring occasionally.

2 Discard the cinnamon stick and purée the fruit in a blender or food processor. Return to the saucepan.

3 Blend the arrowroot with the water and stir into the purée. Bring to the boil and cook, stirring, until thickened. Taste and add more sweetener, if liked.

4 Cool, then spoon into four individual glasses and chill until ready to serve.

PREPARATION TIME:
10 MINUTES

COOKING TIME:
15 MINUTES

CALORIES: LESS THAN 100

Quick Chocolate Mousse

SERVES 4	METRIC	IMPERIAL	AMERICAN
Low-fat whipping cream	*150 ml*	*¼ pt*	*⅔ cup*
Chocolate hazelnut spread	*30 ml*	*2 tbsp*	*2 tbsp*
Brandy	*15 ml*	*1 tbsp*	*1 tbsp*
Ground cinnamon			
Whole strawberries	*4*	*4*	*4*
OR kiwi fruit, sliced	*1*	*1*	*1*

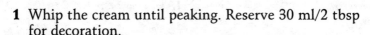

1 Whip the cream until peaking. Reserve 30 ml/2 tbsp for decoration.

2 Fold the chocolate spread and brandy into the remaining cream.

3 Spoon into four demitasse coffee cups. Top with the reserved cream and sprinkle with cinnamon. Chill until set.

4 Place each cup on its saucer with a strawberry or slices of kiwi fruit and a coffee spoon to eat it with.

PREPARATION TIME:
10 MINUTES,
PLUS CHILLING TIME

CALORIES: LESS THAN 100

Fruit Crisp

SERVES 4	METRIC	IMPERIAL	AMERICAN
Can of fruit in natural juice, drained and juice reserved	410 g	14½ oz	1 large
Weetabix	2	2	2
Artificial sweetener granules	5 ml	1 tsp	1 tsp
Low-fat spread, melted	50 g	2 oz	¼ cup
Ground ginger, cinnamon or mixed (apple-pie) spice	2.5 ml	½ tsp	½ tsp

1 Put the fruit in a 1 litre/1¾ pt/4¼ cup ovenproof dish.

2 Crumble the Weetabix and mix with the sweetener, low-fat spread and spice.

3 Sprinkle over the fruit, pressing down lightly.

4 Bake in a preheated oven at 190°C/375°F/gas mark 5 for about 15 minutes until crisp.

5 Serve warm.

PREPARATION TIME: 10 MINUTES COOKING TIME: 15 MINUTES

CALORIES: LESS THAN 200

Quark Refresher

SERVES 4	METRIC	IMPERIAL	AMERICAN
Packet of sugar-free fruit-flavoured jelly (jello)	1	1	1
Boiling water	150 ml	¼ pt	⅔ cup
Cold water	300 ml	½ pt	1¼ cups
Very low-fat quark	100 g	4 oz	½ cup

A few pieces of fresh fruit, matching or complementing the flavour of the jelly

1 Dissolve the jelly in the boiling water. Stir in the cold water and chill until the consistency of egg white.

2 Whisk in the quark and turn into four dishes. Chill until set.

3 Decorate with fresh fruit before serving.

PREPARATION TIME:
10 MINUTES,
PLUS CHILLING TIME

CALORIES: LESS THAN 100

INDEX